4+

Embedding a Culture of Continuous Improvement in Financial Services

Second Edition

Dr Morgan L. Jones, Chris Butterworth and Brenton Harder

Published by Action New Thinking Limited

First published 2017
Second edition published 2018
Copyright © Dr Morgan L. Jones, Chris Butterworth and Brenton Harder

National Library of Australia Cataloguing-in-Publication entry

Creators: Jones, Dr Morgan L.; Butterworth, Chris; Harder, Brenton, authors.

Title: 4 + 1: Embedding a Culture of Continuous Improvement in Financial Services/ Jones, Dr Morgan L.; Butterworth, Chris; Harder, Brenton.

ISBN: 978-0-9873477-3-2 (paperback)   eISBN: 978-0-9873477-4-9

Typesetting and design by BookPOD

All proceeds from this book will be donated to Redkite, an Australian charity supporting children, teenagers and their families affected by cancer, directly or through a family member.

Redkite provides essential support to children, teenagers and young adults with cancer to ensure the best possible quality of life for them and their family – now and into the future. Every child and young person's experience of cancer is unique. To give a child or young person the best chance of managing the cancer journey positively, the whole family and each individual needs to be supported to manage their unique cancer experience. By alleviating the financial and emotional stress and enabling children, young people, their families and their support networks to develop their strengths and skills, Redkite assists the whole family to achieve that positive end.

CONTENTS

CHAPTER 4 EMBEDDING THE HABITS

CHAPTER 5 MATURING THE HABITS

CHAPTER 6 IT DEPENDS ...

ACKNOWLEDGEMENTS

We would like to acknowledge Nigel Adams, John Crossley, Donna Fitzpatrick, Kirstin Graham, Kristen Hansen, Kevan Latty, David Masters, Michelle Lue-Reid, Richard Steel and Richard Young for their valuable comments and feedback on the manuscript, and Professor Peter Hines for his insights. A special thank you goes to Ashley Cooper, founder of Enkohde Pty, for transforming our drafts into professional figures throughout the book and the cover design. Special thanks to Jon Pratlett for his insights on neuroscience and to Dan Bowes for sharing his insights of using the 4+1 Habits in the case study in Chapter 4. Lastly, we gratefully acknowledge the many organisations, senior managers and thousands of front-line employees that we have worked with over the years for sharing their challenges while rolling out the 4+1 Habits in different teams, divisions and organisations.

We have received lots of useful feedback from organisations using the first edition, which has inspired us to develop the second edition. Below are a few examples:

'We have all felt the gratification of successful improvement projects followed by the frustration of grinding to a halt or, even worse, deteriorating back to where we started as we move onto other challenges. 4+1 solves this through the application of simple, effective leadership habits. If you want to remove silos, improve cross-functional teamwork, and create a sustainable culture of continuous improvement, this book is for you, regardless of the industry or environment you work in.'
Scott Miller, Operational Excellence Leader, Mylan Australia

'Our role as leaders is to create an environment that enables our team to be at their best every day and "4 +1 Habits" fits perfectly into this purpose. Our team now has a framework which enables continuous improvement methodology to become part of a way we all believe

and behave. We believe this will ultimately become our cultural and competitive advantage.'

Brett Ashley, General Manager, Countdown

'The 4+1 Habits and behaviours have given us a simple but highly effective framework to implement and embed the Lean way of thinking. We used the original 4+1 book to "articulate" to our wider leadership team the principals of true lean.'

Adam Bentley, National Business Excellence Manager, Countdown NZ

'4+1 is an essential back pocket book for leaders looking to shift their team's or organisation's culture from a "throw the problem over the fence" behaviour to "I have a problem and I am empowered to solve it". When you start to embed the methodologies and tools used in these case studies you start to see the shift in people's attitudes and behaviours. On the back of that, you then start to see a rise in colleague engagement as they feel more empowered to make tomorrow better than today. Written in simple, easy to understand language, this book will assist you to drive the right outcome for your colleagues and customers.'

Stephen Dargan, Head of Process Transformation, BankWest

'Change the culture seems to be the holy grail for any transformation that I have been around. No matter what company or country, the leadership team always states they want to 'change the culture' so that it would be one that the people had continuous improvement and innovation in their daily work DNA. I only saw it happen one time (at GE) before I began using 5 Habits as part of my playbook, and now I have seen it three more times. It is only the thing that makes sense to everyone and really changes the way people think about work, which is the key to the beginning of changing the culture.'

**Jon E. Theuerkauf, Managing Director,
Head of Performance Excellence, BNY Mellon**

ABBREVIATIONS

BPI	Business Process Improvement
BU	Business Unit
CI	Continuous Improvement
CPI	Continuous Process Improvement
CTQ	Critical to Quality
CVP	Customer Value Proposition
DI	Discontinuous Improvement
DMAIC	Define, Measure, Analyse, Improve, Control
FTE	Full-Time Equivalent
FUD Factor	Fear, Uncertainty and Doubt Factor
HR	Human Resources
KBI	Key Behavioural Indicators
KPI	Key Performance Indicators
PBT	Profit before Taxes
PDCA	Plan, Do, Check, Act
SCARF	Status, Certainty, Autonomy, Relatedness, Fairness
SLA	Service Level Agreement
SOP	Standard Operating Procedure
VOC	Voice of Customer
VMB	Visual Management Board

CHAPTER 1

INTRODUCTION

We wrote the first edition of this book to share the lessons we have learned in driving culture especially around the use of habits to embed a culture of continuous improvement (CI) and bottom-up strategy. The feedback from the first edition has been very positive: over 2000 books sold and several thousands of dollars donated to the Redkite charity from sales.

We have received many requests for much more detail on the habits, how to embed them and more examples of their application. We have written this second edition to address these requests and to provide a much deeper understanding of how to bring the habits to life through various stages of maturity.

Many organisations have launched continuous improvement, business improvement, process excellence or Lean Six Sigma programs with varying success. The typical model is to employ an experienced external executive to engage directly with the senior leadership team, develop a deployment plan, train a small cohort of green or black belts, identify and deliver some immediate wins, build momentum with more low-hanging fruit, and hope the top-down approach will permeate the organisational culture due to an obvious display of logic and benefits. Building individual capability of green belts, black belts and sometimes sponsors is a successful approach for creating a proof point that that these methods work within that organisation and its culture.

Figure 1.1 has been adapted from Professor Peter Hines's schematic and shows different improvement approaches employed by organisations. What Hines's research shows is that it is necessary to focus not just on top-down project improvement (DI) but also, at the same time, develop bottom-up continuous improvement (CI) and ensure a focus on end-to-end processes (PI).

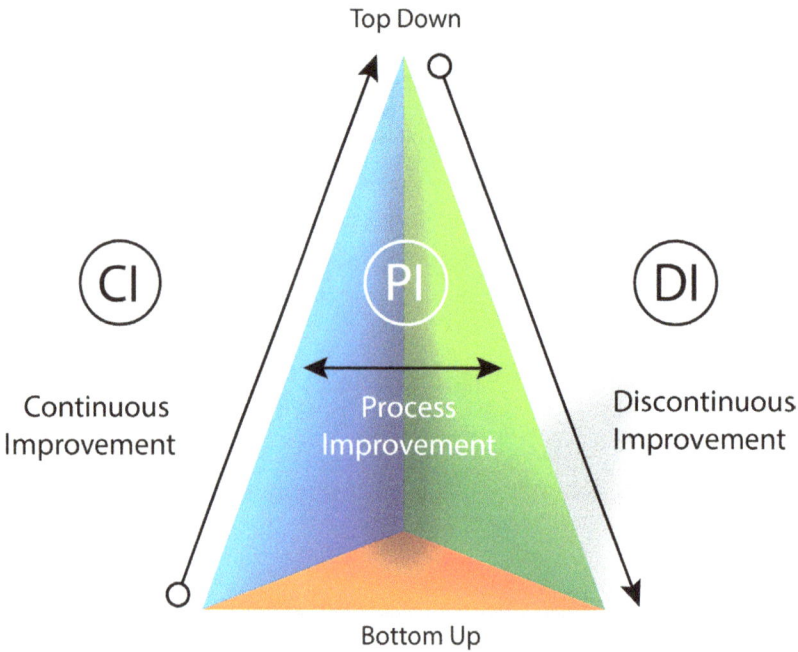

Figure 1.1 Relationship of different improvement approaches

The challenge is that it is estimated that 70% of such deployments fail after five years. Hence, we wrote the first book to share the lessons we have learned in driving culture especially around the continuous improvement (CI) and bottom-up strategy shown in Figure 1.1.[1]

We shared case studies from two major global banks based in the USA and Australia that are applying business improvement and productivity habits to embed a culture of continuous improvement, strengthen individual capability, and execute discrete improvement projects using Define, Measure, Analyse, Improve, Control (DMAIC) thinking. We also introduced the four (4) productivity habits and the fifth (5th) leadership productivity habit, hence the title of our book '4+1'.

We believe that driving change requires an absolute focus on keeping things simple (habits) and understanding the 'why' underlying the tools and techniques that are used to drive the desired outcome. Simply copying ideas from other companies without truly understanding the underlying 'why' merely promotes industrial tourism without achieving the same outcome.[2]

The proven ideas in the first book can be replicated in other financial institutions, other industry sectors, and by governments. They are also scalable across multiple geographies and various organisational sizes. In this second edition, we give more detail about each habit and share a wide range of examples. Our hope is that this book will enable many more organisations to engage their people in driving results through a culture of continuous improvement.

---

1   Satya Chakravorty, 'Where Process Improvement Projects Go Wrong', Wall Street International, 25 January 2010.
2   Mansel G. Blackford, Bridgestone Tyres example in *The Rise of Modern Business*, University of North Carolina Press, 2008.

FINANCIAL SERVICES (FS) FOCUS

The financial services (FS) industry has faced challenges in implementing business improvement methodologies after copying the Lean Six Sigma deployment approaches used by manufacturing and engineering companies during the late 1990s. For financial services, the key challenge is clearly not on how physical widgets are manufactured; rather, the focus is on how people work together to deliver intangible outcomes such as advice and support services.

The service industry sector has been moving towards closer scrutiny of and improvement in customer experience because of rapid changes in customer expectations. Customers' expectations of service levels, response times and personalised experience are constantly increasing. New competitors with new business models are challenging the traditional banks and non-financial institutions such as supermarkets are entering the market with increasingly sophisticated offerings. At the same time, regulatory compliance and scrutiny has increased for the traditional financial service organisations. In short, financial service organisations must increase customer service levels whilst reducing costs and ensuring compliance to regulatory requirements. In this environment, it is critical to develop a culture of continuous improvement to ensure long-term sustainability.

Anyone with a desire to improve the health of their organisation, department or team should read this book. More specifically, the principles, approaches, methodologies, thought-leadership and tools are valuable resources for three groups of people within any organisation – leaders, managers and team leaders, and personnel in the operations and human resources areas.

- Leadership

  » Executives wanting to get more out of their business improvement programs and inspire every employee to not only want to improve the customer experience and thus business results but focus daily actions to *achieve* this while understanding why they are improving

» Senior managers who are looking to create a more responsive/agile business model because of changing customer requirements and expectations

- Managers and team leaders

   » Team leaders or managers responsible for delivering sustainable improvements and savings (human element)

   » Creating a safe and encouraging environment for generating and implementing improvement ideas

- Operations and human resources

   » For creating a sustainable workplace environment and a stable and highly engaged workforce

   » Anyone who believes they want to improve their business improvement skills

TARGET AUDIENCE

Anyone with an interest in deploying Lean Six Sigma within their organisation will get value from reading this book. It has been written for:

- Any financial services organisation – irrespective of size or specialisation or geographic location – that values customers, people, time and resources

- Businesses that are frustrated with their sluggish performance, long lead times and siloed cultures

- Organisations that have tried business improvement initiatives and fallen short or failed

- Organisations looking for sustainability in business improvement rather than simply regular cost-cutting exercises

- CEOs, senior executives, human resources personnel, change agents and leaders in continuous improvement

- Anyone who wants to understand in depth how to apply the habits and the stages of maturity for each one

HOW TO USE THIS BOOK

This book is filled with practical 'what to do' and 'how to do' insights. We reveal the underlying neuroscience that lies behind why a specific tool, method, or approach works. In this second edition, we describe in detail three levels of maturity for each habit and share multiple examples. Finally, we define Continuous Improvement Culture, describe how to measure culture through identifying behaviours, and outline ways to reinforce the desired cultural behaviours using a few targeted habits.

Chapter 2 will discuss the four core habits that have been successfully deployed in several financial services institutions and the fifth leadership habit. We define the habits, describe how they work with each other and reference – from a neuroscience perspective –why each of the habits work, both individually and collectively.

Chapter 3 will discuss how to launch this strategy, and how to begin to embed these habits in an organisation.

Chapter 4 discusses how to lift the maturity of an organisation by embedding these habits, and describe how to continually improve the approach regarding a case study from the Commonwealth Bank of Australia.

Chapter 5 expands on each of the habits and explain how to progress through three levels of maturity from beginner, intermediate and advanced.

Chapter 6 examines how all the habits link together and how they contribute to embedding a culture of Continuous Improvement.

INTRODUCTION TO 4+1 HABITS

It is important to keep the habits as simple as possible. It is very easy to make things complicated and continuous improvement professionals need to avoid complex models that may well be intellectually stimulating but do not help widespread understanding. Keep it simple – if it takes lots of explanation and people do not immediately connect with them, then it needs changing. Always check with a wide selection of people from all levels across the business, not just the continuous improvement team. The **four** core habits are:

1. VMB – Although the Visual Management Board is a tool, the commitment to continually updating it is the real habit. There is also an explicit link to the customer with the integration of the Customer Value Proposition (CVP) which is explored further in Chapter 2

2. Huddles – A short 5- to 15-minute standing discussion around the VMB

3. CI – Continuous Improvement ideas generated by the team, their interrelationships with each other, and their collective power

4. Standard operating procedures result in standard work rules, enabling tasks that are repeatable and reducing the process variation significantly

The +1 habit is Gemba. We refer to this as the leadership habit and it is explained in more detail in Chapter 6. All the habits are linked and are mutually reinforcing. Figure 1.2 is a simple model depicting how the four core and 1 leadership habits link.

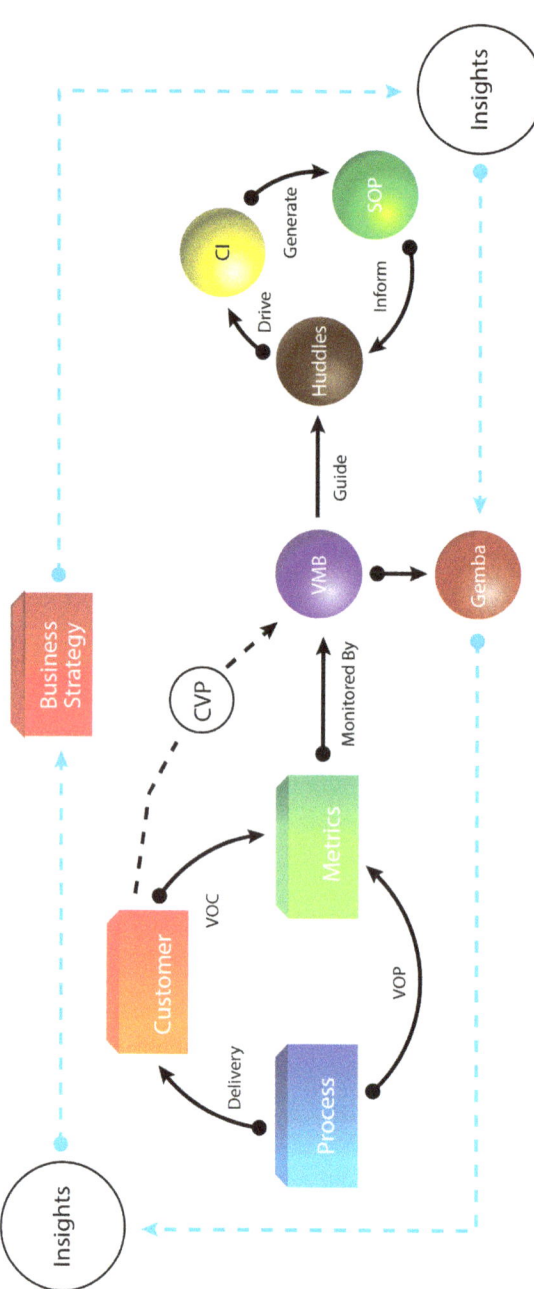

Figure 1.2 Model of the interaction of the 5 productivity habits

DEFINING CULTURE

Culture can be defined in many ways, but for this book, culture is defined as *'a commonality of understanding and interpretation of policies, rules and regulations that result in a consistent set of behaviours of the majority of individuals in a group'*.[3]

The first step is to clearly define the ideal set of behaviours you would like to see employees displaying in the organisation; behaviours that would result in them focusing on the continuous improvement of their roles and tasks to improve the experience for customers and their colleagues. The next step is developing a set of core habits that reinforce and endorse these behaviours. As these habits become embedded, the continuous improvement culture is formed, and everyone's behaviours reinforce the norms of the group thus strengthening the culture.

Figure 1.3 is our CI culture model. It highlights the interaction of culture, habits and behaviours. Our approach of starting with the desired behaviours is aligned to Stephen Covey's second habit of beginning with the end in mind.[4]

---

3   Ronald W. Toseland & Robert F. Rivas, *An Introduction to Group Work Practice*, Allyn & Bacon/Longman, Boston, 2005.

4   Stephen Covey, *The 7 Habits of Highly Effective People*.

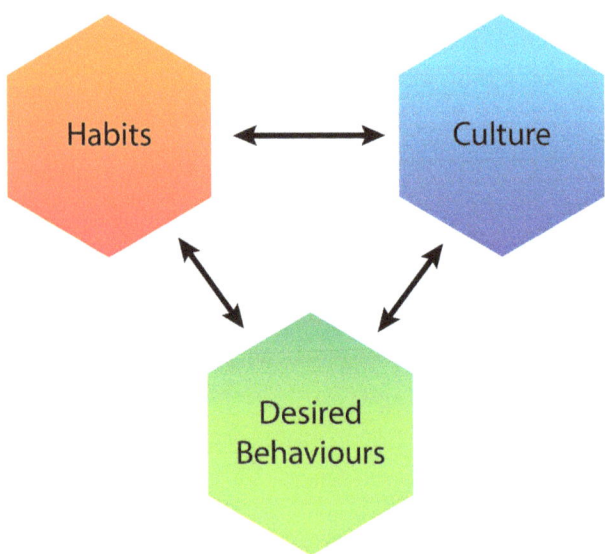

Figure 1.3 CI culture model

Most continuous improvement programs have focused on developing this expertise in specialists such as green and black belts; we refer to this as the building of individual capability. With individual capability build as a foundation, this book focuses on the whole team's attitude and culture. Our suggestion is that it is essential to focus not only on the individual but also on the team and business-wide capability. The habits enable a common language and approach to improvement that is clearly visible in every team and at all levels of the organisation. We achieve this by applying simple tools and techniques to solve small problems when and where they arise. While culture itself is difficult to measure, a simple way of understanding it is to observe the behaviours of individuals in the group or organisational team.

Leaders need to understand that CI cannot be delegated. Rather, it is the leader's job to create a culture of CI in every member of the team and to continually reinforce this. Hence the 5th leadership habit of Gemba walks. Gemba is a Japanese word meaning 'the place where value is created' and a Gemba walk is the opportunity to embed the habits with coaching conversations. Leaders want every employee to be generating ideas to improve the customer and staff experience. And so, the practice of taking Gemba walks is an opportunity to model, and reinforce, the practice of generating enhanced customer experience through interactions between leaders and colleagues.

There is a difference between activities and behaviours and it is the five habits that link these together that will be discussed in detail in the coming chapters.

WHY WE NEED HABITS

To embed a culture of continuous improvement, two key high-level systems need to be designed and implemented across an organisation: a system of improvement and a system of thinking and behaviour. Doing the day job is the system of work, but we need a system of improvement that facilitates and encourages everyone to not only undertake the day job but to constantly strive to improve the way they do their own day job and the process to which they are contributing. We need the system of improvement to be simple and easy to apply across the entire organisation. The system of thinking and behaviour needs to be designed to embed the system of improvement. Designing these two systems is essential to embedding a culture of continuous improvement.

As Figure 1.4 illustrates, these systems are interrelated; however, we see many organisations putting a great deal of emphasis on the system of work with concomitant in-depth standard operating procedures and quality manuals, but failing to design an integrated system of improvement. Thus, it becomes very difficult for people to make changes, for instance improvements to the system of work. This omission leads to lots of work-arounds, lots of frustration and high levels of firefighting.

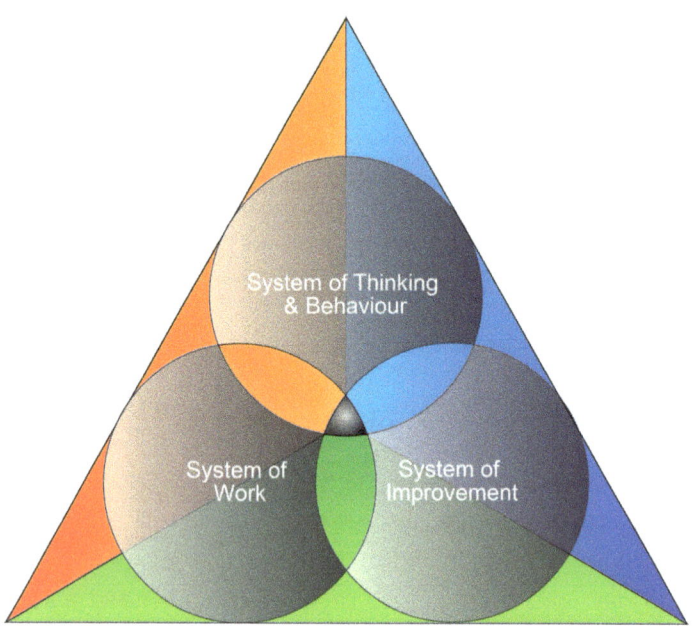

Figure 1.4 Systems of focus (Source: S A Partners)

INTRODUCTION TO THE 4 QUESTIONS

A very simple but effective approach to support the application of the improvement habits is to embed some simple questions that everyone in the organisation can use on a day-to-day basis. These should be worded to match the language and context of each organisation however some examples are given below.

1. 'Are we focused on activities that add value for the customer and the business?'

    This is all about provoking people's thinking to question why are they doing some of the crazy things that frustrate them – often the things they know they shouldn't be doing.

2. 'Are our processes efficient and performed consistently across the team?'

    This is about standardising the things people should be doing, removing and reducing waste and making processes consistent every time they are performed.

3. 'Are we focused on the right activities at the right time with the right skills?'

    This is about understanding customer requirements and the requisite people skills – make sure we get the right people working on the right thing with the right skills at the right time.

4. 'Am I personally contributing to continuous improvement every day?'

    This question brings the other three together with the aim to create an environment where everyone continues to learn and apply the improvement habits. If people use these questions on a regular basis they change the way they look at their work. If the answer to any question is 'no' then there is an opportunity for improvement.

NEUROSCIENCE BEHIND FORMING HABITS

A true understanding of how people's brains work and at the same time, understanding their behaviours is very much critical for creating an alignment to a standard set of behaviours. John Medina[5] and David Rock[6, 7] examined the development and study of habits that drive

---

5   John Medina, *Brain Rules*, Pear Press, 2008.
6   David Rock, *Coaching with the Brain in Mind,* Wiley Press, 2009.
7   David Rock, *Your Brain at Work: Strategies for Overcoming Distraction, Regaining Focus, and Working Smarter All Day Long*, Wiley Press, 2009.

desired behaviours that collectively create a culture of continuous improvement.

1. **The brain is a connection machine** – It is phenomenal at making connections especially around trends in data and targets as well as abstract connections of cause and effect.

2. **No two human brains are alike** – Each of our brains has developed uniquely due to various experiences, external influences and family/societal influences.

3. **Constrained conscious processing capability** – The brain filters the amount of information it requires for processing by using previously formed frames of reference to categorise and remove less important or irrelevant information. Most of the brain's power is in the subconscious part of the brain, where habits are located, whereas conscious thoughts occur in the newer part of the brain, the prefrontal cortex, which by comparison is volume constrained on the brain's processing power.

4. **The brain does not unlearn** – The brain does not unlearn things, except due to medical trauma. The brain creates new neural pathways that drive new thinking and this informs new behaviours. Initially when we are learning new things we must be conscious about the new thing we want to do. This information stays and is processed in the prefrontal cortex or conscious part of the mind. Then, over time, this neural pathway becomes stronger as it is performed repeatedly and eventually moves into the subconscious. A true habit is something we do without having to consciously think about it.

5. **Stressed brains don't learn or listen** – Under stress or perceived danger, blood (containing much of the brain's fuel) flows away from the prefrontal cortex to the major muscle

groups in preparation for fight or flight, reducing the ability of the individual to think rationally, make connections and, most importantly, to listen. In the threat state, the brain's ability to solve problems and collaborate effectively is severely reduced.

A recent discovery that the human brain can change its own structure and function through thought and activity is perhaps the most important alteration in our view of the brain in 400 years. Known as neuroplasticity, it has the power to allow us to change, but it can also lock us into behaviours too. Neuroplasticity has enabled the blind to see, the deaf to hear, the learning disabled to learn, and 80+-year-olds to sharpen their memories to that of 55-year-olds. Norman Doidge's book, *The Brain That Changes Itself*, covers this in detail.

The brain automates everything it can to conserve energy. Change requires vastly more energy to pay conscious attention! An example is learning to ride a bike – we wobble around, fall off and look stupid. It takes attention, practice and correction, and then more practice and correction to move from beginner to competent. Add more practice – up to around 1000 repetitions – and the behaviour becomes automatic due to neuroplasticity as explained in four stages:

- Unconsciously incompetent (unskilled) – You don't know what you don't know. You are unaware of your ability or lack of in relation to a skill.

- Consciously incompetent (unskilled) – You now know what don't know and begin taking the initial steps towards becoming competent.

- Consciously competent – You can demonstrate the skill, but it requires your full attention and is very effortful. You will be using your prefrontal cortex or PFC (just behind your eyes, which is the most recent 'add on' to our evolving brain) and this part of the brain is very energy demanding. The brain consumes around 20% of our body's available energy and yet it weighs only around 1.5kg.

- Unconsciously competent – This fourth stage is like riding a bike without having to think about it, and possibly chatting with a friend at the same time. There are different levels within each stage and at the unconsciously competent stage you might be proficient, an expert or a master for example. Now instead of engaging the PFC (the energy guzzler), the basal ganglia which is far more energy efficient takes over.

Is it any wonder that many people resist change in the early stages? However, dealing with change is much easier if you can predict what's ahead (the brain desires certainty so being able to predict what lies ahead allows it to feel safe). Safety is the brain's number one priority. It's much easier to predict what's ahead when you have a model in your head and you can assess where you are and where you are heading. Neuroplasticity is in action whether we like it or not, either reinforcing/locking in behaviours which become unconscious habits, which either serve us or don't, or through self-directed neuroplasticity, allowing us to choose and make the changes we want to make, initially through massive practice and correction.

What single change about your thinking or behaviour will you now work on to take advantage of self-directed neuroplasticity?

A child learning to play piano scales for the first time is a good example. She tends to use her whole upper body – wrist, arm, shoulder – to play each note. Even the facial muscles tighten into a grimace, but with practice the budding pianist stops using irrelevant muscles and soon uses only the correct finger to play the note. She soon develops a lighter touch and if she becomes skilful, she develops grace and relaxes when she plays. The demand drops from a massive number of neurons to an appropriate few well matched for the task.

This more efficient use of neurons occurs whenever we become proficient at a skill and explains why we don't quickly run out of (neural) map space as we practice or add skills to our repertoire.[8] Trained neurons fire more quickly, process faster and recover quicker, ready to fire again. Faster neurons = faster thoughts, a crucial component of intelligence, and vital for the pace we are challenged to operate at today.

Plenty of practice of the new behaviour is required, with appropriate increases in complexity, to move from self-conscious novice (consciously incompetent) to expert (unconsciously competent).

So, in relation to the new behaviours and habits you want to develop and utilise, are you prepared to do what it takes to go from where you are to where you want to be? Will you put in place support systems that encourage you to meet your commitment to practice, be open to mistakes and correction, and apply any new learning?

CHAPTER TAKEAWAYS

- The four main themes:

1. Culture is measured through behaviours

2. Simplicity increases likelihood of success

3. CI requires team and business capability as well as individual capability

4. Customer experience is becoming a primary focus of all

- Plus 1

5. **Habits embed behaviours**

---

8   Norman Doidge M.D., *The Brain That Changes Itself*, Penguin Books, New York, 2007.

CHAPTER 2

THE HABITS

FIVE PROVEN HABITS

One of the most effective ways to create and embed both the system of improvement and the system of thinking and behaviour is to select a small number of key tools and embed these as daily habits. These habits are not necessarily the same for every organisation and need to be context-specific; however, the tools selected are most likely to include a focus on structured problem-solving, visual management and continuous improvement. The five habits introduced earlier for financial services organisations are:

1. **VMB** – Visual management board

2. **Huddles** – The short conversations that take place at the visual management board

3. **SOPs** – Standard operating procedures that document the current best practice and provide the baseline for future improvement

4. **CI** – Continuous improvement: striving to make tomorrow better than today while ensuring a better experience for customers and simplifying the process for one another

5. **Gemba** walks – The opportunity to embed the habits through coaching conversations

However, it is not enough to create a system of improvement. Just giving staff some simple and effective tools, and good training in how to use these tools, will have mixed results. The early adopters will pick them up and exploit their potential but eventually their use will fade away and be remembered yet another flavour of the month. So, for the system of improvement to become a habit, it is essential to support this with the system of thinking and behaviour.

Leaders and managers also need to understand how their roles will change. Leaders and managers at all levels need to not only understand the system of improvement, but they need to be able to lead by example and coach other staff members in its use. The table below shows the difference in the time that people spend in a typical day working on each system depending upon the level of maturity of the continuous improvement culture.

The reactive level identifies where improvement is individually led in isolated pockets by leaders or teams who have taken personal initiative but there is no business-wide standard. The formal level is where a business-wide standard has been defined, but its implementation is limited to isolated islands of excellence which may well be very mature but the standard has not been adopted business-wide.

At the deployed stage, the system of improvement is well established and can be found throughout the organisation, whilst at the deployment stage both the system of improvement and the system of thinking and behaviour are well established – autonomous, in other words.

The habits have been fully deployed and behaviours that support them clearly established. At way of life, both systems are so well embedded in the organisation's culture that it is evident in every team and leader and has become the way that the business operates on a day-to-day basis. At way of life level, organisations would be expecting to be at the level required to challenge for a Shingo prize.[9]

---

9   See www.shingo.org.

	Reactive			Formal			Deployed			Autonomous			Way of Life		
	SoTB	Sol	SoW	SoTB	Sol	SoW	SoTB	Sol	SoW	SoTB	Sol	SoW	SoTB	Sol	SoW
Leaders	10	20	70	10	30	60	20	40	40	40	40	20	60	30	10
Managers	5	10	85	10	20	70	10	30	60	20	40	40	20	50	30
Associates	2	0	98	2	10	88	5	15	80	5	15	80	5	15	80

SoTB - System of Thinking & Behaving   Sol - System of Improvement   SoW - System of Work

Table 2.1 Percentage of time spent working on each system (Source: S A Partners)

As the table above illustrates, leadership time needs to be focused on establishing the system of improvement, and then demonstrating and reinforcing the ideal behaviours to support it. Where this is not done, we see leaders and managers being very busy working at one or even two levels below that which they should be. We observe lots of firefighting with leaders, managers and associates complaining of long hours and being too busy to work on improvements.

The starting point for the system of behaviours is for leaders to define the culture they wish to see in the organisation. If this is not addressed, then many different cultures evolve as determined by local leaders or just strong personalities at any level. To quote Edgar Schein,[10] a professor at MIT Sloan School of Management:

'The only thing of real importance that leaders do is to create and manage culture. If you do not manage culture, it manages you, and you may not even be aware of the extent to which this is happening.'

The only way to determine culture is through observable behaviours. Thus, defining and constantly reinforcing behaviours that support the system of improvement is one of the most effective ways to ensure it becomes a sustainable habit. The behaviours are strengthened through practising the habits, and the habits are reinforced through practising the behaviours. Examples of behaviours for each habit are given in this chapter.

1 VMB – VISUAL MANAGEMENT BOARDS

The VMB is at the heart of the habits providing the focal point for teams to review performance, set priorities, solve problems and manage continuous improvement activities. It is both a tool (i.e., a visual management board) and a habit (i.e., the use of the VMB as

---

10   Edgar Schein, cited in Ch. 19, *WCOM (World Class Operations Management): Why You Need More Than Lean*, Carlo Baroncelli and Noela Ballerio (eds), Springer, 2016.

it is continuously updated with performance data, progress on CI activities, team specifics, and customer experiences). Unfortunately, whilst they are easy to install, many teams struggle to sustain them.

It is useful for any organisation to review some of the more common issues observed and experienced so that the likelihood of long-term sustainability can be increased by addressing these. This reflection on our lessons learned and some of the things observed elsewhere resulted in a list of traps to try to avoid. These include for example:

- The VMB just becomes wallpaper containing masses of pretty graphs that take hours to produce but no one obtains information from, or uses in any meaningful way

- The VMB is used as just a one-way communications board – a one-way update created for the boss or visitors with little interaction and few, if any, agreed actions

- The VMB is the 'boss's board' – produced by the team for the boss so he/she can monitor what's happening but creating more work and little benefit for the team. Sometimes it is even created by the boss for the team which results in no relevance to staff and little engagement.

- The VMB is used as a single tool not linked to others, and not integrated into the management process

To improve the chances of success and increase the probability of long-term sustainability, the VMB needs to be an essential element of the system of improvement – not just a tool but the central habit that drives and supports all the others. It must be useful to the team and owned by them.

To help achieve this, the biggest chance of success comes if teams are enabled (at all levels) to develop their own VMBs. This can be difficult for leaders to accept but an essential part of team engagement is the ability of the leader to let go and allow the team to experiment with their own VMB. This is not about abdicating responsibility – 'go forth and make a board' – but rather about setting the right context, the purpose and the 'why' and then leading by example. One way to think about it is as an experiment. The board starts with a few simple ideas and evolves through regular cycles of Plan, Do, Check, and Act (PDCA).

t a high level, the organisation should be trying to achieve two things with the VMB:

1. An alignment of the team to True North and customer value, and

2. The team's engagement in proactively wanting to deliver these.

Too often the VMB is heavily focused on alignment with measures and targets deployed to the team with little or no explanation of the 'why'. In many cases the layout of the VMB, the measures and even the entire content are given to the team. While alignment is very important, an exclusive focus on this limits engagement. It is engagement that is critical to sustainability and truly creates a habit rather than just encouragement of using a tool. Engagement with the VMB comes through involvement and ownership in its design and content. The VMB becomes the team's VMB when the 'why' and the high-level 'what' are fully explained and the team can create their own VMB to deliver on the 'how'. So instead of a manual of templates, a company standard format and detailed audit system around the completion of the fixed boxes, it is far better to communicate a loose 'standard' that ensures sufficient alignment and supports lots of engagement. The approach should be to make the standard very short and simple:

•   the VMB must be clearly linked to True North and customer value;

- it must contain measures and targets that demonstrate these links;

- it must contain actions linked to measures;

- it must contain CI activities linked to True North and customer value.

When approached this way, the response is often remarkable as teams can apply a high degree of creativity. Instead of being told what to have on their VMB, they decide for themselves. While every board may look slightly different, the key elements are always included, and this approach also means that great ideas are rapidly copied and improved upon by other teams. Both the content and the use of the VMB is continuously improving – measures and targets and activities change as progress is made, customers and their needs are better understood, and new challenges are set. The VMBs also drive the other habits as they provoke discussion on areas to focus upon, for example:

- Opportunities for CI

- Updates for SOPs embedding CIs and general process updates

    » Pictures of customer experiences and team successes

    » Examples of mini-lessons learned on specific topics

- The specific Customer Value Proposition (CVP) for the team (a CVP is the high-level reason why your business matters to customers. It describes what your customer wants, and provides people in your business with direction and a common understanding on how to behave to deliver value to the customer)

- Metrics to measure the CVP

- Business metrics (leading and lagging) and targets

- Actions to achieve targets

- Workload predictions

- Customer feedback

- Improvement areas and action plans structured around a PDCA cycle

- Team specifics – holidays, capacity.

The VMB needs to be used not as a stand-alone tool but an integral part of the management operating system. Meetings around the board should follow an integrated sequence with timings linked to customer and business cycles of activity. These meetings are called huddles and these are the second habit.

Example behaviours

- Associates or front-line employees – Regularly update the VMB with real-time information

- Managers – Ensure that the 'what' is clear and regularly confirm the team's clear understanding of the purpose.

- Leaders – Set clear expectations about VMB content and explain the 'why'

 *Ask two simple questions to test the effectiveness of a VMB. These questions can be asked by anyone at any level and are especially powerful if regularly asked by leaders across the organisation. They are not intended as a test of the person being asked but rather a test of the effectiveness of the strategy deployment system and the effectiveness of the VMB to link people to strategic and customer priorities.*

1. *Do you know what the key goals are for our business over the next couple of years?*
   (This question is checking for alignment.)

2. *What are you going to do differently to help achieve these goals?*
   (This question is checking for engagement.)

2 HUDDLES

A VMB is only as good as the quality of the conversation it provokes. The times of meetings are planned, fixed to a set time and agreed in a sequence which facilitates cross-learning and enables leaders to be present at more than one meeting during the day. The frequency and timing are determined by the operating rhythm of the team. Many teams have the time of the huddle prominently displayed on the VMB. It holds them accountable and lets others know when that team will be unavailable. It also flags discussions that may be of interest for others to attend.

The duration of the huddle is fixed and typically takes a maximum of 10 to 15 minutes. Teams need coaching and guidance on how to make best use of the time and a couple of simple tips can be very useful: for example, the one-minute rule. If a topic is highly relevant to just two people rather than the whole team, then they have a maximum of one minute to discuss it. Any more than that, the discussion must be taken off line and the answer agreed outside of the huddle.

Some teams find it useful to have a clock with 15 minutes marked in red, and some teams decide to have penalties for people not prepared or who turn up late. It depends on what works for each team. The key is that the focus is action-oriented and the team gets value from the discussion. There is a standard agenda and a guide to standard practice for running a huddle. For example, the standard practice could include rotating leadership/facilitation of the huddle amongst different team members for each meeting. Some teams may choose to have a published timetable of who will lead the meeting and when. Others may select the leader of the huddle discussion randomly; some vote and others use a variety of different approaches. It does not matter how they arrange the huddle if the 'why' is clearly understood.

For example, leaders should not try to dictate a standard of how they must rotate. Rather, explain that it is a standard and then explain why rotating is useful. For example, 'sharing the facilitation helps embed learning and understanding and is developmental for the team and the individual. How you do it is up to you.'

Leaders need to be coached in the standard practice around running huddles: for example, how to ensure the whole team are contributing, what type of questions to ask and what not to do. Everyone has their own style, so rather than make the standard practice overly regimented it is better to agree on a few simple principles and behaviours.

A good huddle should:

- Be short and focused

- Review recent performance against targets

- Celebrate successes

- Agree on priorities

- Agree actions with clear owners and dates and document these on the board

- Be facilitated by different members of the team

- Be set to take place on a fixed time and day

- Be sequenced to the operating rhythm of the team

Example behaviours

- Associates – Contribute proactively to the huddle discussion.

- Managers – Regularly attend huddles to listen, learn and support the team.

- Leaders – Frequently demonstrate that the huddles are important by visiting them and asking about them.

One test that is always useful to apply is to check if the teams are now spending less time in meetings than they were before the implementation of VMBs and huddles. Make sure to review the current list of meetings and get rid of most of them. Ask why isn't this meeting subject covered in the huddle? Don't just add huddles on top of the existing meeting structure.

3   CONTINUOUS IMPROVEMENT

The third habit is continuous improvement (CI) – striving every day to improve the customer experience while making the process simpler for ourselves and our colleagues. There is a very strong link between CI, the VMB and the huddles as these helps to identify opportunities and set priorities. Too often CI improvement activities are driven by what an individual feel is important. It may be a great improvement but not necessarily the greatest priority for the scarce resources that are available. Making CI a habit and linking it directly to the VMB ensures greater alignment to business priorities. It is also very powerful for engagement as teams see that their improvement activities are valued and having a positive impact on them, the customer and the business.

CI also needs to operate with a simple framework, and one of the most effective is Plan, Do, Check, Act (PDCA) to encourage widespread adoption across all levels. The PDCA cycle keeps things simple and makes it relatively quick and easy to implement a CI idea whilst at the same time ensuring a standard structure is followed.

Many organisations try to force-fit either PDCA or DMAIC (Define, Measure, Analyse, Improve and Control) to everything. Instead it is more effective to use both as appropriate and make it clear they are applied to different activities. Therefore, PDCA may be used for CI activities, whilst DMAIC is used for significant projects typically supported by certified Lean Six Sigma green and black belts. In other words, PDCA is used for continuous improvement (bottom-up) and DMAIC is more useful for discontinuous improvement (top-down) projects. As Professor Peter Hines illustrates in the model below, both CI and DI are required – it is not an either-or choice.

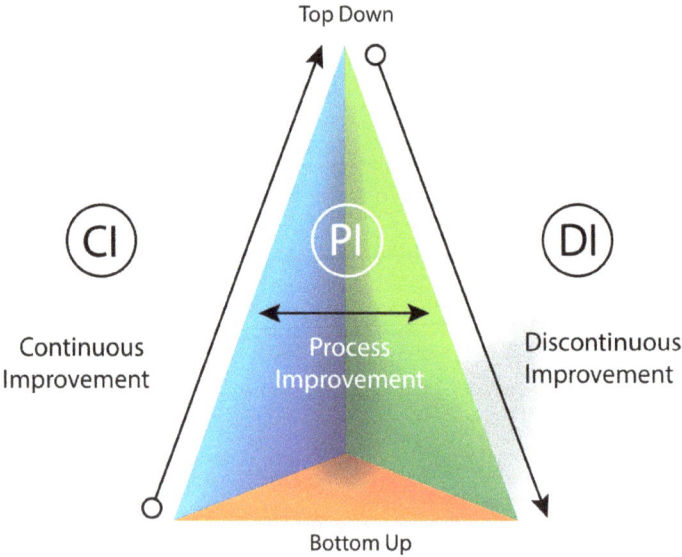

Figure 2.1 Relationship of different improvement approaches

Simple problem-solving tools such as '5 Whys' and fishbone diagrams are taught to everyone and integrated into the PDCA cycle. There is another link to the VMB with teams not only identifying the opportunity from the data on the VMB, but also tracking implementation actions and displaying '5 Whys' and fishbone templates on the VMB. Structured problem-solving is embedded into the CI habit and explicitly linked to the PDCA cycle. For example:

- Plan – Always create collaboratively and agree together on the problem statement

- Do – Use fishbone diagrams and '5 Whys' as appropriate to establish the root cause(s). Dividing into several teams to add DeBono's six thinking hats can encourage even more creativity and rigour around the possible solutions. Use a PICK (Possible, Implement, Challenge, Kill) matrix to agree on the optimum solution(s) to implement.

- Check – Test the solution(s)

- Act – Fully implement, standardise the current optimum solution, communicate, celebrate success and roll out to other areas

A critical aspect of the CI habit is the reward and recognition system for implementation of improvements. These are in place at team, department, division and whole business level. Lots of small-level and frequent recognition is far more effective than a massively bureaucratic process that rewards only a select few. The improvements also need to be tracked with an effective but simple cost-benefit analysis which produces value-driven benefits, societal benefits and performance-driven benefits for all staff of an organisation.

Example behaviours

- Associates – Regularly identify continuous improvement opportunities that both improve the customer experience and make the process more efficient.

- Managers – Coach and encourage the application of PDCA and structured problem-solving by asking questions about the problem-solving process that has been used to arrive at the solution rather than question the solution.

- Leaders – Ensure the system for managing CI ideas implementation is simple and enables fast and frequent feedback and recognition.

Ensure leaders set the expectation that they want everyone (including themselves) striving to always improve rather than settling for the status quo. It's important to make it clear that people have been recruited not just to do the job they have but more importantly to continuously improve the way the job is done. The expectation is that everyone contributes

to improving the experience for customers and making the process simpler for each other.

4 STANDARD OPERATING PROCEDURES – SOPs

SOPs provide the baseline standard from which improvement can be measured and implemented. Whilst they are critical for many reasons they are often viewed as necessary evils used to police compliance. They are often overly complicated, difficult to locate and out of date. As such, they become discredited and a source of frustration resulting in people performing the process despite the SOP rather than it being a useful tool. A phrase heard too often is 'if I followed the process we would never get the job done on time'. A good SOP will facilitate and accelerate process performance rather than be an onerous complication.

In order to address these issues, it is necessary to ensure that people understand why SOPs are a useful source of support, not something to blow the dust off just because the auditors are coming! Key to the success of this habit is to really get to the heart of 'What's in it for me?' by moving away from regarding SOPs as a compliance evil and developing the attitude that SOPs are a useful 'single source of truth'. Some simple principles may help:

- Keep the SOP simple

- Ensure that the people doing the work are involved in creating the SOP

- Use visual aids such as pictures, screenshots and simple flowcharts

- Make the SOP an integral part of the improvement process

- Ensure new starters are trained using the SOP

It is useful to develop some simple questions that can help people to understand the power of SOPs:

- How do you know what is the best way to execute this process?

- What is the standard for this process?

- How do you know if suggested changes will improve the current process?

- How do new starters get trained in the standard process?

The intention is for a SOP to be the 'single source of truth'. Rather than inhibiting the process and necessitating lots of 'work-arounds,' the SOP needs to become the single best way to get things done. It is the best way today, but it also provides a base from which to improve further. In other words, it is used to support continuously improving the standard. Some of the best SOPs contain the time and resources required to undertake the process, enabling the rapid quantification of any proposed changes.

Another useful way to think of SOPs is to apply the key points from TWI (Training Within Industry).[11] While it's not necessary to explicitly use this terminology it is very useful for building in the four core elements of the approach:

- Job instructions

- Problem solving

- Learning on the job, and

- Job methods.

---

11   Donald Dinero, *Training Within Industry: The Foundation of Lean*, Productivity Press, Portland, Oregon, 2005.

It is critical to establish a simple process and clear ownership for managing and updating SOPs. They need to be easy to find and easy to keep up to date. It is useful to create visual 'how to' one-point lesson guides coupled with the SOP which are used as a quick reference and memory jogger. SOPs are integrated into the continuous improvement cycle, and a key step before an improvement can be implemented is that the SOP has been updated to reflect the change. All new starters are trained using the SOP as it is used as the basis for induction. Equally importantly, it is also used as the basis for upskilling as people are promoted or move to a different team.

Example behaviours

- Associates – Make regular use of SOPs, contribute to their creation and keep them up to date as improvements are implemented

- Managers – Ensure that people are trained using the SOPs and understand why they are important

- Leaders – Ensure that the system to manage SOPs is simple and easy to use, e.g., ensure easily accessible, easily updated and changes are easily implemented and communicated.

 *Keep the SOP as simple as possible with process flow charts and pictures/screen shots, and avoid trying to cover every possible thing that might go wrong. Instead focus on the main flow and make it part of the SOP that people stop the process and seek guidance when something happens that is not the norm.*

Figure 2.2 illustrates how SOPs fit into the other habits. The conversations in the huddles are about the gaps between the metrics and targets on the VMB. This identifies potential areas for improvement, some of which will logically fall into a CI suggestion using

PDCA while others will be just 'do it' activities. Once the teams come up with a solution, they 'lock it in' with a simple process improvement and modified/updated SOPs. The team is notified at the next team huddle of a SOP upgrade/change.

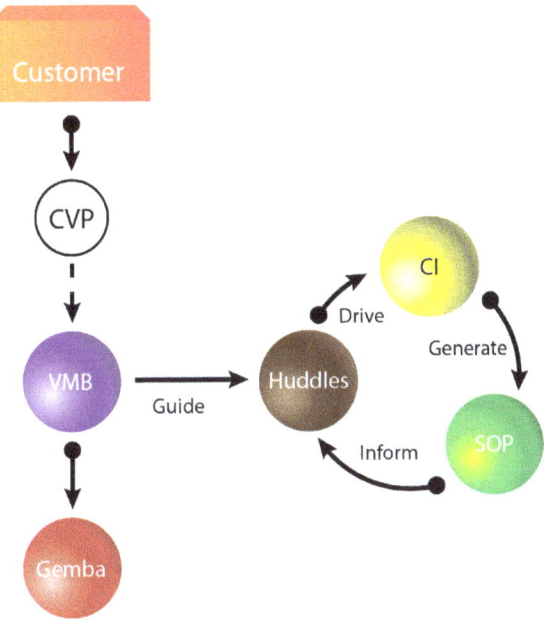

Figure 2.2 The four habits working together

5   GEMBA WALKS

At the Commonwealth Bank, the decision was made not to introduce this habit at the same time as the other habits as it was felt that people needed to understand and practice the other habits first. This approach is not cast in stone and is entirely context specific, to be discussed and decided on as part of the implementation planning. In the case of the Bank of New York Mellon, all five habits were rolled out at once in an attempt to better integrate managers as 'owners' of the daily routines and habits. While the early introduction of Gemba walks was helpful, without additional training and incentives the introduction was less than effective. Unfortunately, both a carrot (manager buy-in and participation) and a stick (manager KPIs to ensure the managers are doing the walks) were needed in that case.

Gemba walks provide the opportunity for leaders to understand how well the organisation has embedded the habits, and provide the opportunity to test the effectiveness of the deployment of the systems of improvement and thinking and behaviour. They are in no way meant to be used to test or assess the individuals or teams visited but rather test how well the systems have enabled the desired knowledge and behaviours. The Gemba walks are intended to support, promote and check on the other habits. With limited understanding and application of the other habits it was felt that introducing Gemba walks from day one risked discrediting them. Leaders needed a deeper understanding of the other four habits before they could undertake effective Gemba walks. Also, teams needed time to learn and practice the application of the first four habits.

With hindsight, it was found that another advantage of introducing Gemba walks later was that it provided the opportunity to reinforce the other habits and make it clear that they were here to stay. The Gemba walk is not intended as a management audit. If teams feel they need to prepare for a Gemba walk this is a clear indication that there is an issue with both the system of improvement and the system of thinking and behaviour that needs to be addressed.

The walks provide the opportunity for meaningful discussions, with the leaders spending far more time actively listening and observing rather than giving advice. Leaders need to demonstrate curiosity, 'I am here to learn about the process and understand how well we have deployed the habits'. An indicator that the walks are working well is when teams experience the Gemba walk as the leaders supporting them rather than trying to catch them out. Leaders need to remember that the Gemba walk is not the opportunity to be a superhero! We do not want the approach to be one of 'tell me all your problems and I will go and get them fixed'. Rather, the appropriate perspective is that it is an opportunity to teach people how to fish for themselves rather than just keep giving them a fish.

The Gemba walk is not:

- The 'royal tour' with lots of hand-shaking and kissing of babies

- 'Management by walkabout', but involves a lot of observing and listening

- An opportunity to catch people out

- A pre-prepared script with a set list of questions

The Gemba walk is:

- The best way to truly understand what's happening

- A process to coach and develop people's skills by recognising that the role of leaders is to serve the workforce to better enable the workforce to serve the customer

- A opportunity for first-hand engagement and cultural health check

- An opportunity to check the True North cascade and understanding

- A practice that is learned by practising

- The Check in the high-level Plan, Do, Check, Act (PDCA)

An effective Gemba walk will leave leaders, managers and associates feeling valued. For associates and managers, the target condition is that they feel respected as a result of the Gemba walk. It should result in a greater sense of ownership and pride in the job they do. For leaders, the Gemba walk should give a better understanding of the process and any issues, and should lead to much stronger working relationships. It is the opportunity to serve, coach and give recognition. Many leaders initially struggle with Gemba walks. Typical initial reactions to the idea of a Gemba walk include comments such:

- 'I already walk the floor every day.'

- 'I am too busy with getting the job done to spend time walking about.'

- 'We have real-time data systems that tell me everything I need to know.'

To address these concerns, it is essential that leaders are trained in why a Gemba walk is useful and what its purpose is, and are given the opportunity to practice in a safe environment. A few simple questions can be very effective to encourage leaders to think about why a Gemba walk is useful. For example:

- What defines value for our customers?

- Where does that value get created?

- Who are the people that create that value?

- How can I best serve them so they can serve the customer?

Providing a simple and quick reference guide to support leaders and using a 'buddy system' for 360 feedback are also very useful. The 'buddy system' in this case works by two people who work together agreeing to observe and give feedback on each other's behaviours and interactions. Five key points for any Gemba walk:

1. Make a positive difference with every Gemba walk

2. Observe and learn

3. Be curious, not interrogative

4. Show respect and humility

5. Always follow up

Where leaders spend their time demonstrates what is important to the organisation. Gemba walks are key to supporting both the system of improvement and the system of thinking and behaviour.

Example behaviours

- Associates – Ensure that their workplace is always 'Gemba walk ready', i.e., they do not need make any special preparations for a Gemba walk

- Managers – Demonstrate that every conversation (not just formal coaching sessions) is an opportunity to develop people through enquiry-based coaching

- Leaders – Recognise that every conversation is an opportunity to listen and learn

Figure 2.3 displays the relationship between the Gemba walk and the 4 +1 Habits.

Key to understanding customer needs is gathering Voice of the Customer (VOC) that allows one to derive a consistent and strong Customer Value Proposition (CVP).

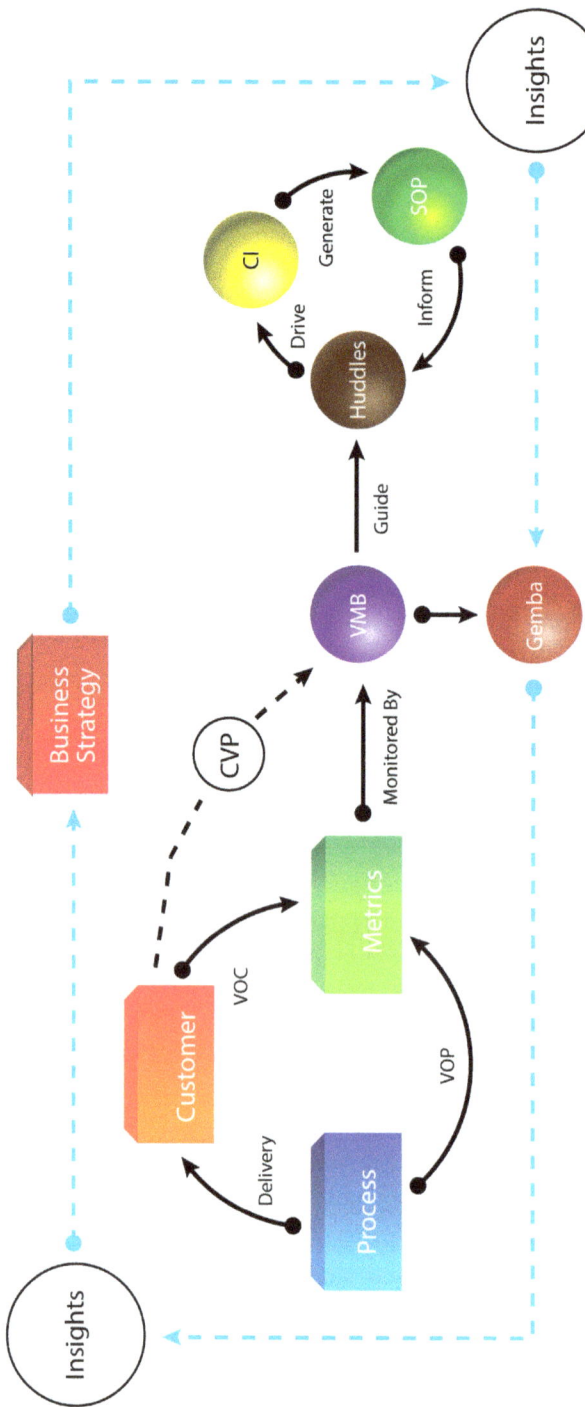

Figure 2.3 The overall interactions of 4+1 Habits

42

NEUROSCIENCE BEHIND 4+1 HABITS

Let's look at the five habits discussed in detail above and understand why they work both individually and with each other:

VMBs – The brain is a connection/association machine. The act of updating the VMB and making the information visual allows others to make connections. Data visualisation – whether quantitative or qualitative – speeds up the processing of information within the brain by a factor of 3-4 times. It also increases the possibility of insight.[12] No two human brains are identical as our brains change due to various experiences, outside effects and family/societal effects. Displaying data visually minimises the likelihood of people drawing different conclusions from the data depicted.

Huddles – Human beings are social creatures by nature. Creating safe spaces for people to celebrate wins, acknowledge one another, ask clarifying questions, share and constructively evaluate ideas, in a group setting, can support and optimise team members' brains. Feeling safe and supported (even when challenged) allows the brain to direct blood flow to the prefrontal cortex enabling the individual to better attend, focus, listen and interact and create the conditions to facilitate insight.

One way of thinking about how to create constructive social interactions is to use the SCARF model by David Rock[13] that can help to make those interactions and more specifically 'huddles' more successful. Science is now showing that social pain, the pain of feeling rejected for example, shows up in the same area in the brain as physical pain. Unlike many other motivational theories, the SCARF model is quite modern and SCARF is an acronym, where the letters are taken from the first letters of the words:

---

12   Duclerci Sternadt Alexandre & João Manuel R. S. Tavares, *Introduction to Human Perception in Visualization*, 2006.

13   David Rock, SCARF Model, *NeuroLeadership Journal*, 2008.

- **Status**, which is about feelings of the relative importance of self to others.

- **Certainty**, which concerns being able to predict the future.

- **Autonomy**, which provides people a sense of control over events.

- **Relatedness**, which is a sense of safety and belonging with others.

- **Fairness**, which is a perception of fair exchanges between people.

Behind all this is the idea that a person's brain will activate behaviours to minimise perceived threats and maximise rewards, and that the brain reacts in the same way to social needs as to our primary needs like food and water. So, if a stimulus, for example, a huddle, is associated with positive interaction, positive emotions and rewards, a person will probably move towards it physically or emotionally. But if it is associated with negative interaction, negative emotions or punishments, it will be perceived as a threat and the person will probably move away from and avoid it. That all sounds pretty straightforward.

The SCARF model can be used to plan the set up and running of huddles in such a way that threats are minimised and rewards are maximised in each of the five areas (or domains, as they're called) of Status, Certainty, Autonomy, Relatedness and Fairness.

If a person feels that they are being threatened, their emotional brain – particularly the amygdala – will work quickly to protect them, instigating the flight/fight response, thus reducing their ability for rational thought, to make good decisions, to solve problems, and to collaborate – which are the things we want teams to do.

What makes the SCARF model so useful is that it identifies the five domains that activate the primary reward or primary threat circuitry in a person's brain.

CIs – Building on the principles of 'the brain is a connection machine' and 'no two human brains are identical', the group can apply some simple tools and basic structure to take advantage of the different ways of seeing issues, making new connections as a collective, and solving business problems identified on the VMB and huddle.

From neuroscience research, the following is a summary of the impact of making information visual. As the VMBs mature, they should become more visual.

- Almost 50% of the brain is involved in visual processing[14]

- 70% of all your sensory receptors are in your eyes[15]

- We can get the sense of a visual scene in less than 1/10 of a second[16]

- Researchers found that colour visuals increase the willingness to read by 50%[17]

- People following directions with text and visuals do 323% better that those people following directions without illustrations[18]

---

14   E.N. Merieb and K. Hoeh, *Human Anatomy and Physiology*, 7th edn, Pearson International, 2007

15   E.N. Merieb and K. Hoeh, *Human Anatomy and Physiology*, 7th edn, Pearson International, 2007

16   R. Green, *The Persuasive Properties of Colour*, Marketing Communications,1998

17   W.J. Levie & R. Lentz, R., *Effects of text illustrations: A review of research*, Educational Communication and Technology, 1982

18   W.J. Levie & R. Lentz, R., *Effects of text illustrations: A review of research*, Educational Communication and Technology, 1982

CHAPTER TAKEAWAYS

- The four main themes:

1. Habits must be measurable

2. VMBs are not just tools

3. Huddles must be integrated into the business operating rhythm

4. Leader's role is to develop people through curiosity

- Plus 1

5. **The right habits drive the right behaviours**

CHAPTER 3

IMPLEMENTATION

Consider employee habits as the 'muscle memory' of an organisation, and that the collective sum of such habits largely dictates the way an organisation interacts with their customers, suppliers, regulators, and internally with each other. Repeated day after day with little thought or reflection, habits are a deep-rooted network of routines and behaviours. Good habits and behaviours generally lead to good outcomes, just as bad habits and routines can lead to bad outcomes. Trying to improve performance outcomes means making employees stronger by building muscle memory through the introduction and implementation of good behaviours and routines.

The introduction, implementation, and sustainability of a program built around the 4+1 Habits begins with a collective desire to change, requires a robust implementation plan, and must have a logical alignment to organisational goals and objectives in order to succeed.

ilure rates are quite high for transformation initiatives that do not follow a prescribed method for properly engaging and involving the organisation to enable sustained change.[19] There are a variety of implementation plans available, but the key is to focus on the core aspects necessary to effectively address employee behaviour and change day-to-day habits:

1. Desire to change

2. Sponsorship

3. Communication planning

4. Training and coaching plan

5. Resistance management plan

Changing habits takes time, and success won't come overnight. In some cases, it may even feel as if an organisation is actually going backwards as it begins to see how collectively bad or ineffectual habits have weakened organisational muscle memory. Building new muscles and new habits is hard and takes time and commitment. The organisation needs to believe that the effect of not changing is far worse than mustering the energy and effort it will take to change and improve. Once started, it needs to stay the course and avoid being tempted by other projects or initiatives. Just as 'yo-yo dieting' doesn't work, neither does 'yo-yo 4+1 Habits'.

Benefits also take time to accrue. With patience, the cumulative sum of many small incremental improvements efforts made every single day across the organisation can generate millions in savings, improved customer service, and significantly reduce risk. But these benefits come only when employees are empowered to change and improve themselves through a well-sponsored and structured implementation plan.

---

19   John P. Kotter, *Leading Change: Why Transformation Efforts Fail*, HBR OnPoint, 2000.

NEED FOR CHANGE

According to John Kotter, most change or transformation initiatives begin when some individuals or groups start to look at an organisation's competitive situation, market position, technological trends, and financial performance.[20] It's natural to breathlessly react at a decline in revenue, drop in performance, or new regulatory challenges. While such factors may establish a sense of urgency and be a call to action, improvement efforts are improperly focused on reacting to the output rather than addressing bad habits that may be the root cause.

Many of the performance improvement programs and efforts of the last two decades were developed simply as a desire to change. Without knowing exactly what or where improvements were needed, organisations would hire black belts and change agents to focus on the link between the voices of customers and process output, and enlist and train teams to use a variety of quality improvement methodologies and tools to measure, analyse, improve and control process output. Unfortunately, according to Satya Chakravorty, while such programs might generate considerable excitement and noise, 60% failed to yield lasting and sustainable change – gradually momentum was lost and the organisation fell back into old habits.[21]

According to the Boston Consulting Group, perhaps the high failure rate was due to a narrow focus, primarily on cost reduction and efficiency. While such activity normally has a degree of initial success, most of the gains will turn out to be short-lived and ethereal. Instead, forward-looking organisations embrace a 'lean that lasts'[22] philosophy that instils a comprehensive and sustainable program of change with a focus on employee engagement, client centricity, and continuous improvement grounded in the day-to-day behaviours and habits of an

---

20   John Kotter, 'The 8-Step Process for Leading Change', http://www.kotterinternational.com/the-8-step-process-for-leading-change/, 2017.

21   Satya Chakravorty, 'Where Process Improvement Projects Go Wrong', WSI, 25 January 2010.

22   BCG, *Lean that Lasts – Transforming Financial Institutions*, September 2012.

organisation. Employees are active and self-interested participants driving gains and identifying means to achieve them through a culture and structure that are optimised for performance and decision-making.[23]

Employees want to deliver high-quality products and services to their customers, so the only way we can ensure lasting and sustainable change is to give them the permission and training to change themselves! Teams need to 'see' what they do and how they deliver every day on their visual management boards. They need to see how their actions make a difference in the lives of their customers, and they need the opportunity to come up with new ideas to continuously improve what and how they deliver. Employees need to feel empowered and in control of what they do every day, and management needs to listen, too. Working together, teams and managers will incrementally change a workplace in fundamental ways.

A truly lean company is one with a natural focus from bottom to top, aligning resources with a common strategy.

IMPLEMENTATION PLAN

A successful implementation plan must emphasise the employees' role in the identification and ownership of continuous improvement ideas, as well as management's role in engaging and empowering teams. As stated earlier, implementation activity must follow a series of phases and steps that will provide the visibility and process clarity to both employees and managers.

The following pages contain an example of an actual Board-level implementation plan with clear alignment of resources to strategy.[24]

---

23   BCG, as above.
24   Brenton Harder, Actual plan submitted to Executive Committee in support of a 4+1 program (scope and scale modified for illustration purposes).

Value at stake

Productivity is a capability that must be developed and sustained across the company. The Productivity program is expected to deliver an incremental sustainable annualised profit before taxes (PBT) of between $Xm and $Xm in three years.

Background

- At the last Executive Committee, the formation of the Business Productivity Improvement team was announced with a focus on improving productivity and establishing it as a capability across the company. We have made a public commitment to deliver Productivity benefits and embed Productivity as a capability.

- Productivity involves continuously improving everything we do and it includes improving our processes, reducing errors and re-work, eliminating waste and ensuring we get value from whatever we use or purchase. It is also about making it easier for our people to do their jobs and for our customers to do business with us.

- Productivity in the company is not intended to replace our Sales and Service methods and it is not about expense management through mass redundancy or offshoring existing work.

- The company has had an association with Lean and Six Sigma methodologies under previous quality programs for nearly a decade. Where applied, significant benefits have been achieved; however, variable commitment from leaders in the company has led to inconsistent application and poor embedding of the capability. Nearly X00 projects have been completed with more than X000 FTE completing a Lean Awareness training program, and more than X00 FTE have participated in a Lean project. Despite this training, behavioural change is only evident in a few areas.

- There has never been a top-down public commitment to a company-wide program before, although we have had a focus on costs.

- Productivity in the company uses established practices drawn from Lean and Six Sigma methodologies to create Process Excellence.

- We have embedded risk management and controls as an integral part of the methodologies. Business process owners (who are accountable for risks in end-to-end processes) and/ or operational risk staff are involved in projects.

Objective and approach

- The Productivity program has three main objectives: to establish productivity in the DNA of the organisation; to deliver efficiency and productivity outcomes across the company; and to sustain and enhance our commitment to customer service. It is expected to deliver an estimated benefit of PBT between $Xm and $Xm.

- Our approach has a number of distinguishing features that leverage existing capabilities to maximise the chance of success. We will utilise the full Process Excellence toolset in major end-to-end process transformations and we will use Lean, a subset of our tools and methods, to improve the efficiency at a local workplace level.

- To drive fundamental change, the Executive Committee has agreed on five Productivity Habits as a basis for cross-company engagement. It is intended that all divisions will embed these habits in the organisation. 'How to' guides, templates and other learning materials are also being developed. The agreed minimum habits are:

» Visual Management Boards

» Huddles (to be established simultaneously with Visual Management Boards)

» Continuous Improvement

» Standard Operating Procedures (SOPs)

» Gemba walks.

- Three coaching models will be deployed to introduce, implement, and sustain the Five Productivity Habits across the company:

  » Bespoke coaching: 1 Business Process Improvement coach engages 1 to 3 teams

  » Group coaching: 1 BPI coach engages department

  » Business Unit (BU) coaching: 1 BPI coach trains 3 BU coaches followed by each of the BU coaches engaging 3 teams (1:3:9 ratio)

- Lean has been selected as it can be effectively applied in a manner that allows us to scale the program across the company. The Lean tools and techniques are readily learnt and can be utilised widely by our staff without the need for an understanding of statistical methods. Lean includes mechanisms for continuous improvement and replicating best practice and the behaviours. Lean is compatible with, and reinforces, our Sales and Service culture, and is well suited to changing the mindsets and behaviours of our leaders.

- We are using a central team (BPI) to drive the program. The role of this team is to:

  » Execute and deliver benefits with the BUs through projects;

  » Transfer skills and capabilities from the practitioner to business leaders;

  » Enable BUs to be self-sufficient through training and subsequent coaching;

  » Challenge the BUs to ensure that as wide a set of benefits is achieved as is practicable and cultural change is achieved;

  » Complement those BU-specific gains with cross-BU transformational changes;

  » Establish mechanisms that transform the culture and embed the changes through five habits coaching and training, and;

  » Maintain and improve our productivity methods and practices.

- This team is built on the previous Process Excellence team and comprises skilled Lean/Six Sigma practitioners. We have XX black belt equivalents in the BPI team and an additional XX in the broader business. The team must move from being an internal consultancy, supporting a demand-driven model across a few business units, to a systematic whole-of-company delivery model with a mandate to drive change.

- The BPI team includes X senior business unit representatives (BU Lead) whose role it is to co-ordinate, challenge, drive and champion the establishment of productivity as a capability within each BU. They work with the BUs to identify, scope, prioritise and schedule the projects that will ensure the program covers all key processes and staff. They will be grouped into two teams, Distribution and Services, each led by a senior experienced Productivity Director.

- Delivery resources have been centralised and managed as a pool to be applied to the BU and cross-BU projects and this function will include a small program management office function to track and schedule BPI project resources, BU project resources and other skilled and trained delivery staff.

- Two support functions are required. A Change function is responsible for communications, training, coaching and accreditation and to ensure we embed the desired cultural change. A Finance function is being used to track the effectiveness of the overall program and to report on the benefits and improvements in productivity across the company. This role leverages the existing BU finance support teams.

- To avoid contention in IT project delivery and with subject matter experts, the program will use two complementary approaches, Lean projects and Transformational projects.

- Lean projects focus on natural workgroups and utilise a structured approach to reorganise work, standardise work practices, reduce/remove errors and re-work, embed visual management of performance, embed a focus on continuous improvement, document processes and embed local cultural and behavioural change that supports productivity. They may span organisational boundaries and are staffed by a combination of BPI resources and BU resources. Initially BPI resources will lead the Lean projects but as leaders are developed in the BUs as part of the project rollout, the BPI staff will move out to focus on the large cross-business unit transformational initiatives and coaching leaders within the BUs, leaving the BUs to be self-sufficient in continuing the Lean rollout.

- To embed productivity into the culture of the organisation a number of change management activities will be undertaken including:

  » Active sponsorship by the CEO and Executive team.

  » Recognition of successes and achievements in regular messages from the CEO and company executives.

  » Establishing Process and Productivity metrics in CEO, Group Executive and Executive General Managers reporting packs and linking improvements in the metrics to KPIs.

  » Establish a KPI for team managers to maintain minimum standards of Lean management after any Lean project. (Note: A balanced scorecard approach with Customer Service and Risk will be needed to ensure we do not forsake the customer or risk management practices.)

  » Integration of the recognition of Productivity into the CEO Awards.

  » Integration of Productivity/Process Excellence into management and leadership behavioural frameworks.

  » Integration of Productivity language into our existing Sales and Service frameworks and utilisation of the Sales and Service coaches to support and emphasise productivity. This includes the use of daily planning to manage workplace resource utilisation and allocation, weekly meetings to discuss continuous improvements, and visual displays of performance.

» Widespread training and upskilling.

Current status

- As cultural change takes time and is difficult, the engagement between the BPI program and each business unit varies.

- To rapidly scale up the Lean projects we have prioritised BPI delivery resources on the following initiatives:

  » Plans have commenced to leverage two company-wide topics before the end of the calendar year (May/June and September) to emphasise 'right first time, every time' and 'no waste' as key drivers of productivity.

  » Through April and May key process productivity metrics will be embedded in management reporting packs across most business units. Throughout May discussions will occur to link productivity metrics to KPIs.

  » Through May the multi-year Lean rollout program will be detailed and planned to assess demands on business resources and identify any additional skill or capability gaps.

Reporting and measures of success

- We will report quarterly to the Board: Total Income per FTE; Sales per FTE; Employee expense/Total Income; Customer-facing FTE to Back-office FTE; Cost-to-income ratio; the financial benefits generated by the program; the extent to which the program is changing the behaviours of our staff;

and the progress of the major projects. We will report each half-year to the market on selected productivity metrics.

- The primary outcome metric will be the productivity gained (realised or reinvested) through the elements of the program and the delivery of an incremental PBT of between $X and $X. If benefits are reinvested appropriate sales or revenue productivity metrics will be established to monitor the return from that investment.

- Secondary measures of program success include:

  » The extent to which our staff experiences a Lean project in their local team. The target is to cover 90% of our staff.

  » We will train 90% of our managers.

  » Ongoing certification will be an important element of the program.

  » Significant change in the importance and commitment to productivity in internal surveys. The baseline for this will be determined in the current People and Culture Survey.

  » Embedding Productivity in leadership behaviours and HR systems.

  » Inclusion of Productivity in the CEO Awards to recognise outstanding individual and team achievements on this important capability.

SPONSORSHIP

There are only two types of projects in any organisation: those that senior management cares about and all the rest! And of course, driving change through implementing 4+1 Habits must be at the foundation of ANY organisation that truly desires lasting change. Regardless of the change methodology, if the habits and behaviours of the organisation are left unimproved, there will be no lasting change.

Effective sponsorship is frequently cited as the number one contributor to any project's success. This includes active and visible ownership of the 4+1 initiative and active participation in all facets of deployment. Kotter reinforces the need for creating a powerful 'guiding coalition'[25] that goes beyond senior management to include thought leaders and resources known to drive change and innovation. Engaging various levels of management and employees ensures depth and breadth of commitment and ownership, as well as tie-in to strategic and human resource planning.

Effective sponsorship means that senior leaders walk the talk. They lead by example by huddling with their teams in front of their VMBs and drive timely and significant continuous process improvements at both the strategic and tactical levels. They leverage SOPs to manage the business, and rely heavily on Gemba walks to truly understand and appreciate what is really going on across the organisation. They eliminate organisational friction by making 4+1 Habits a required way to do business, and expect the entire organisation to do as they do.

Senior management also knows that many little improvements made daily across the organisation add up to big and lasting change. Minutes saved by improving a four-person operational process, a customer better served by a six-person support team, or a regulatory issue solved by improving a reporting process all add up and combine to make things simple and easy for customers and each other. Little improvements made every single day can accrue millions in savings, improved customer service, and significantly reduce risk.

Sponsorship is important at all levels of the organisation, especially within the 4+1 Habits programs. Local champions can be put in place

---

25   John Kotter, 'The 8-Step Process for Leading Change', http://www.kotterinternational. com/the-8-step-process-for-leading-change/, 2017.

to ensure consistency at both a site or process level. While these 'local champions' may not have hierarchy control, they do command control at logical control levels.

COMMUNICATION

- Communication should be a natural extension of effective sponsorship, but must also be planned and managed for maximum effectiveness. This begins with a simple message that is repeatedly carried over and over again through multiple media and channels across and within various organisational divisions.

An example of simple messaging:

Productivity is making things simpler and easier for our customers and each other. It makes good sense and it's becoming a way of life across the company.

All facets of the 4+1 initiative should be a part of everybody's daily dialogues, and everybody should have a clear understanding of his or her role. Effective messaging goes beyond coffee mugs and mouse pads to build consensus and understanding of the need for change, and a compelling path to get there. Making a change is a personal choice. No matter what senior leaders believe, employees will not change unless they want to change. Therefore, communication must resonate and get to what employees care about and value. To gain support, a good communication plan must provide a compelling case for how employees will be better off by embracing 4+1 Habits. Answering 'What's in it for me?' (WIIFM) early and often in all forms of communication avoids the very common mistake of under-communicating by a factor of ten.[26] In many cases, good

---

26 Kotter, John, 'The 8-Step Process for Leading Change', http://www.kotterinternational. com/the-8-step-process-for-leading-change/, 2017.

transformation plans can fall far short of expectations simply by poor or inconsistent communication. Messaging can fall victim to the day-to-day noise inherent in any organisation, or simply be misunderstood by recipients.

Every chance that management has to address the use of 4+1 Habits must be leveraged and woven into the fabric of the communications plan. Management must also understand that actions speak more loudly than words. Managers should 'catch' teams huddling and should participate in discussions. They should start any visit by attending a team huddle, and ask employees about their level of engagement, share their feedback, and ask questions. All it takes is for one employee to see a manager inspecting a VMB for word to get around that management cares!

Employees should also be involved by sharing stories and anecdotes about their huddles and VMBs on internal social media or intranet chat rooms. Floor competition and 'huddle crashing' are natural follow-on activities of active teams. Such activity can encourage an end-to-end view of the way work flows from team to team across a floor, and can even add to common dialogue regarding metrics and customer requirements.

In initial implementation, training and communication plans should be closely linked to ensure branding and messaging are the same, not similar. This means that the look and feel of any training material should be exactly the same as any video or communication material produced and released to employees. While the goal of the program is to introduce a lingua franca (common language) based on customer delivery, the program must be allowed to 'flex' to accommodate different divisions or departments as the speed of adoption and buy-in varies from department to department.

TRAINING AND COACHING

An accessible and fun example of an effective training and coaching plan focused on building new habits is the 1984 American movie, *The Karate Kid*.[27] In the movie, young Daniel learns karate through repetitive chores and seemingly mundane exercises taught by Mr Miyagi. Repeated and practiced every day, Daniel unknowingly develops the habits and muscle memory necessary for success on the karate mat!

Such a training and coaching plan is not so far-fetched, as many quality programs such as Six Sigma or Lean suffer from terminology baggage that can be unfamiliar or confusing to employees. Technical jargon, foreign-sounding words, or esoteric philosophies may feel out of place in some organisations, thereby adding an unnecessary layer of confusion to the training and coaching of employees. Mr Miyagi found a way to introduce intricate karate moves to young Daniel by teaching, practicing, and embedding familiar moves and processes in an unthreatening and sometimes entertaining manner. The 'muscle memory' learned from continual practice (and feedback) allowed Daniel to learn karate without knowing it, just as employees may learn continuous process improvement without getting bogged down with non-value-added technical terms.

A good training and coaching plan will involve a variety of media and delivery platforms to ensure employees receive training at the proper rate and mode to secure maximum understanding and turn-around. A particular helpful technique is to leverage existing processes or protocols that can easily adapt or bolt on 4+1 Habits. Sales & Service processes normally have some form of regular sales meetings (huddles) using a dashboard (VMB) and dynamic sales plans that change according to dashboard metrics. Standard operating procedures are usually in place and used, as well.

---

27   *The Karate Kid*, Columbia Pictures, 1984.

Training refers to a scheduled session involving a dedicated instructor or teacher imparting knowledge about how to do something, or cause someone to learn or understand something by example or experience. Coaching is more of an ongoing series of interactions or conversations to allow a team to self-discover solutions after they have received initial training.

An effective training and coaching program leverages both techniques by introducing relevant and applicable training in a just-in-time manner to allow employees and teams to use new tools and skills to address the day-to-day issues and problems that can pop up across an organisation.

Training involves:

- Introductory video – Normally delivered via some form of HR learning platform to all employees and serves as a basic introduction and 'what good looks like' example of all 4+1 Habits. The video should be fast-paced and light with several examples of live teams demonstrating effective 4+1 Habits.

- All-hands training – Normally linked to the video and delivered on demand, simple training introduces basic tools and techniques that employees can use and leverage on a just-in-time basis. This training normally goes beyond the 4+1 Habits to include seven basic quality tools useful in team-based problem solving and innovation.

- Template repository – Available templates for VMBs, SIPOC (Supplier, Inputs, Process, Outputs, Customer) SOPs, and ROI calculation tables posted in a public folder and referenced heavily in both the introductory video and all-hands training.

- Examples repository – Pictures and videos of other VMBs, SOPs, and huddles available for teams and employees to see 'what good looks like', and compare their team against others.

Executive presentations should leverage this repository and make an example of some of the more innovative or textbook examples.

- Onboarding training for new employees – Delivered to ALL new employees to ensure they have a full understanding of the 4+1 Habits and are aware of the expectation of engagement and participation.

- Manager training – An essential ingredient to any program, frequently overlooked as early training focus is normally on grass-roots employees (team level) and executive or senior management. Somehow middle managers get lost in the early phases of the program and left out of training endeavours. This is a big mistake as much of the friction encountered in change programs comes from middle managers that may feel threatened by programs that seemingly interfere with their management models.

- Refresher training – Multi-year programs should consider having some form of annual retraining or re-engagement to provide the chance to upgrade the program, introduce new training material, or present advances to the strategic thrust of the program. Such training can also introduce more advanced concepts such as Business Process Management (BPM), Lean Six Sigma, Activity Based Costing (ABC), or any number of modules focused on statistical process control (SPC).

Coaching can be delivered in four ways:

- Bespoke coaching – Normally delivered by a single expert (green belt or black belt) to one to five teams in eight to ten sessions. This provides the greatest level of consistency and engagement, but at considerable cost due to the hands-on engagement of individual coaches with small teams. The coach would provide scheduling, administration, and assorted support for the teams, in addition to day-to-day coaching.

- Group coaching – A single expert (green belt or black belt) engages an entire department or site to ensure multi-team consistency and repeatability. Similar to the Bespoke coaching model, coaching would include eight to ten sessions, but delivered to much larger, multi-team groups. The coach also provides scheduling, administration, and assorted support for the teams.

- Business Unit coaching – A single expert (green belt or black belt) engages and trains with three coaches selected by the business to deliver coaching using either the Bespoke or Group coaching model in a ratio of 1:3:9 – one coach trains three coaches who each trains/coaches three teams. Scheduling, administration, and assorted support can come from either the coach or business support.

- Virtual /Online coaching – On-demand coaching available either synchronously or asynchronously via an online learning platform/chatroom.

Regardless of the chosen method, time is required for the teams to customise and make the 4+1 Habits their own. They need time to personalise and integrate the routine into their daily and weekly rhythm, as well as personalise VMBs and SOPs to match their department or team standards. It is important to remember to strike a balance between the need to adhere to any and all corporate standards versus customisation to maximise engagement. Too many standards can stifle organisational creativity and buy-in, but too much freedom makes it difficult to grow consistently and evenly, as well as to share best practices.

An important element to any training and coaching plan is the idea of team accreditation to recognise, assess, and continually improve an entire organisation's 4+1 Habits program:

- Recognition – Recognise teams that have achieved significant business maturity and capability using 4+1 Habits, basic quality tools, and performance benefits.

- Change management – Assess coaching quality delivered and sustainability of embedded changes.

- Continuous improvement – Provide teams with a self-assessment report to identify usage, consistency, and the basis for an action plan to bridge any gap to further develop team maturity.

- Maturity assessment – Allow teams and the organisation to compare and track capability across all five habits. A Productivity maturity assessment grid provides teams with the ability to gauge increasing progress (scale of 1-5) for each of the 4+1 Habits:

Scale	Basic			Intermediate	Advanced
	1	2	3	4	5
Visual Management Boards	There are no visual displays such as posted metrics, performance metrics etc	Visual displays exist, but are often not regularly updated or used effectively to take action	Visual displays are understood and track meaningful performance indicators. Trigger points that require intervention are set for formal corrective action	Visual displays are implemented and maintained by teams. The displays are the primary tool for communication of current status, planning & evaluating performance	Every aspect of the performance measures, KPI, action items, KBI, and meetings are displayed in the team area under standard formats designed by the team
Team Huddles	Not happening anywhere	Sporadic meetings with no set agenda/ structure or timing	Normal daily/ weekly scheduled meetings with set agenda, but agenda does not focus on key segments of VMB	Normal daily/ weekly scheduled meetings with set agenda, huddles carried out around VMB	Daily/weekly meetings occur with set agenda and everyone standing around VMB. Team quickly responds to changing demands
Continuous Improvement	No Continuous Improvement initiatives anywhere	Continuous improvement initiatives triggered, but there is little action taken on submitted suggestions and as a result , low participation	Continuous Improvement activities occur, but they are random and not tied to business or team objectives	Continuous Improvement tools used to identify improvement opportunities, small improvement opportunities identified and implemented	All process improvements are driven by using Continuous Improvement tools, high impacting opportunities identified and tracking of benefits implemented
Standard Operating Procedures	No Standard Operating Procedures exist	Standard Operating Procedures exist, but they may not be current, complete, used or existence not known	Standard Operating Procedures exist, however they may not be followed consistently	Standard Operating Procedures exit, they are generally followed and occasionally updated	Standard Operating Procedures exist. They are consistently followed as well as reviewed and updated regularly
Go Gemba	No Go Gemba events done or Go Gemba done not in accordance with Gemba Planning Guide	Go Gemba done by team leader and as per Gemba Planning Guide	Go Gemba conducted at team leader +12 level across multiple processes and as per Gemba Planning Guide	Go Gemba conducted at Team Leader +1, +2 and +3 levels across multiple processes as per Gemba Planning Guide	Go Gemba conducted at all levels including senior management and as per Gemba Planning Guide

Figure 3.1 The productivity maturity assessment grid

67

Accreditation programs can take on a Bronze, Silver or Gold motif to track the progress of teams as they develop further capability and deliver information to the continuous learning of the organisation:

- Bronze – The entire team has completed all training, implemented at least one continuous improvement idea that has delivered X minutes saved, and scored three or more on self-administered capability survey.

- Silver – Six months of demonstrated behaviour at Bronze, significant process engagement and behaviour, clearly developed proactive metrics and links to customer critical-to-quality requirements (CTQs), and a score of four or more on self-administered capability survey.

- Gold – Six months of demonstrated behaviour at Silver level with significant recorded benefits and savings, leading best practice assessed at four or more on self-administered capability survey, and clear thought leadership and contribution to the growth and development of the overall performance excellence community.

Accreditation programs can become an important part of both the annual strategic planning process (KPIs), as well as the HR development process:

- Strategic planning – Setting organisation-wide goals (KPIs) to grow the overall capability is an important win derived from any 4+1 Habits program. The first year of implementation might be focused at the team level, and designed to have all teams operating at Bronze level within 12 months. Subsequent years could have a certain percentage of teams at Silver or even Gold levels of capability within 24 or 48 months.

- HR planning – Management may want to include Bronze, Silver or Gold team ratings in the development of goals for managers, and require certain standards for bonus or promotion consideration.

RESISTANCE MANAGEMENT

Change is disruptive to any organisation, and any program of change, no matter how small, should expect to encounter some form of resistance at any point during implementation. Even a program such as 4+1 Habits, involving minimal risk and cost, may encounter some resistance.

Resistance planning should consider mitigation for both proactive and reactive impediments, including:

Business case

- Cost – Implementation costs for a large, organisation-wide 4+1 Habits implementation can range from near zero to well into the millions of dollars when all factors are considered. If an initial 'splash' is intended through training and implementation, program costs for videos, on-demand training, and other expenses (including materials, training, and travel), can add considerable cost to the program. Organisations should consider the cost of producing VMBs for distribution versus homemade VMBs using available white board or conference room space. Costs for employee or coaching travel can be considerable in the early days of implementation, but should also be budgeted throughout the life cycle of the program.

- ROI – Return on investment is a function of the program benefits divided by the overall program costs. Some organisations may have an internal ROI hurdle that would be difficult to substantiate for 4+1 Habits programs due to the incremental nature of some of the early savings, and returns from training employee engagement are next to impossible to quantify in monetary terms.

- Changing market/regulatory environment – External environments have less impact on the program itself. They are more of a concern to the organisational focus as it is sometimes difficult to stay committed to a change program in the face of dramatic market moves or regulatory pressures. As previously mentioned, it is sometimes too easy for an organisation to lose focus and program momentum. Start-stop-start programs make it difficult to properly engage staff and management commitment.

- Business commitment & buy-in – Different departments have different expectations and levels of capability; therefore, some departments may have greater rates of acceptance/resistance based on employee capability, management commitment, and/or resource availability.

- Legal/regulatory – Similar to changes in market/regulatory environment, there may be legal impediments to involving certain customer information in a public forum (huddle), or cross-border data sharing issues for non-local teams.

Planning

- Resource availability – Most of the resource resistance will most likely come from managers trying to hold back employees from participating in training out of concern for time away from processing or servicing. Until 4+1 Habits becomes part of the rhythm and behaviours of the team, any program will need to balance the 'required' versus 'voluntary' nature of the initiative. Obviously, if HR or compensation goals are tied to the program, more attention is likely.

- Complexity – 4+1 Habits is not rocket science, nor should it be. The entire philosophy is to simply empower teams to own their own continual improvement in delivery to the customer.

- Development time – It's better to launch something that is not yet perfected than it is to wait until it's perfect. There will always be inconsistencies in change initiatives, and not everyone will agree with the approach. Trying to develop material that will appeal to everyone will only cause delays in benefit realisation. It is far better to get the material and program into employees' hands as soon as possible to allow them to own and develop the program at their own pace.

Organisational

- Cross-functional involvement – Organisational-wide implementations will mean that the program progresses at different rates in different organisational units. Some teams are more capable and have more resources to dedicate to initial efforts, meaning a higher level of buy-in and earlier recognition of benefits. Other areas of the organisation may take more time to come up the learning and execution curve, delaying benefits and impeding natural growth and evolution. In this case, the use of a local champion is helpful to build rapport and community around a single site or building as opposed to different teams. Some operations and distribution centres may have a variety of teams and divisions housed in one location. Rather than implement at the team or division level, it may make more sense to implement at the site level with a local champion to oversee the rollout. If the organisation is building green belts or some other form of Productivity Practitioner, this is also a source of community to achieve cohesion and engagement.

- Process ownership – Some organisations are structured and managed at the process level. Similar to the example above, it may be most expeditious for the process owner to also 'own' the 4+1 Habits introduction and implementation across his or her process (regardless of the various business units involved). The contiguous nature of work across a process makes implementation of 4+1 Habits a natural way of working and easily adopted to process management.

- Multiple locations for implementation – Disparate locations are initially a difficult deployment issue as in-person training and engagement is not possible. This tends to slow the adoption of VMB usage and ownership without the use of online or shared folders. The idea of a huddle is reduced somewhat when dealing with time zone differences or even language issues.

- Change management issues – Keeping the huddle and continuous improvement ideas up-to-date on a VMB should not be too difficult when executed properly. The VMB should be a natural extension of the team(s), and any and all changes are done in the spirit of team progress

Technical

- Technology experience – Very little technology is normally involved in the methodology or tools associated with 4+1 Habits implementation; however, interaction and integration with organisational technology infrastructure may be required when deploying remote VMBs, training platforms, or distributed training and coaching.

- Scope changes/options – These must be kept to a minimum with as few options as possible. Multiple choices deplete energy. There is a certain beauty in simple choices that provides a common denominator and common language across the organisation.

- Knowledge of business processes – Such knowledge adds both a high degree of credibility and mobility to coaches, as they are able to take on the role of player/coach, meaning they can leverage their own experience and knowledge of the business area to further speed the development and integration of 4+1 Habits into the organisation. Knowledge and subject matter expertise also allows coaches and teams to integrate better with thought leadership and management to ensure buy-in at all levels.

- Quality methods, skills and experience – Green belt and black belt level experience is normally a prerequisite before a coach can engage or train a team, not so much for the required technical knowledge but for the experience that normally goes along with certified quality practitioners. Quality experience also provides a more proactive just-in-time ability to introduce tools or methods as they are required or encountered in a process.

External

- Vendor/contractor experience and support – While it is preferred to have in-house capability for training and coaching, it is also possible to augment staffing in early phases to fill gaps in locations or departments where more training and/or coaching is required. Due to the relatively simple material, experience is the preferred ingredient, and organisations should look for contractors that have experience in 4+1 Habits coaching. Many contractors would prefer to work on projects that require extensive analysis or senior management engagement, in which case, programs of this nature are not for them.

- Multiple vendors – In those instances where contractor support is to be provided in place of in-house practitioners, it is preferable to leverage a single vendor to eliminate the administration of separate contractors and contacts.

ALIGNMENT TO STRATEGY

Mark Twain is famously quoted as saying that he's in favour of progress, but it's change that he doesn't like, and for many employees, this spectre of change produces what's called the FUD Factor – Fear, Uncertainty, and Doubt.[28] They lose certainty, the comfort of the known and the familiar, as well as losing a sense of competency, financial security, and sense of control. As such, employees must be persuaded that the gains will be greater than the losses if they are to embrace the change.

Establishing whether the 4+1 Habits program is voluntary or mandatory is the first consideration and an essential starting point to alleviating the FUD Factor. While there are advantages and disadvantages to both, there is little debate that required participation would most likely get more attention and co-operation than a voluntary program regardless of the corporate culture, and go a long way to moving the organisation to action. Linking corporate goals, business unit strategies, and individual objectives to the 4+1 Habits initiative is an essential starting point to creating clarity of purpose and removing uncertainty.

Clearly establishing key performance and implementation goals ensures that the initiative is not just 'corporate speak' and that all layers of the organisation are on the hook for the success of the program. Employees are encouraged to participate in the solution, thereby building greater buy-in and faster take-up of the newly introduced behaviours and habits. Managers are more involved because they know they are expected to contribute and manage in a new way.

---

28   Willie Pietersen, *The Journal of Business Strategy*, Columbia Business School.

Examples of alignment to strategy include:

- Analysis of the following information – Total Income per FTE; Sales per FTE; Employee expense/Total Income; Customer-facing FTE to Back-office FTE; Cost-to-income ratio; the financial benefits generated by the program; the extent to which the program is changing the behaviours of staff; and the progress of the major projects – will display alignment progress.

- The primary outcome metric may be the productivity gained (realised or reinvested) through the elements of the program and the delivery of an incremental PBT of between $X and $X. If benefits are reinvested appropriate sales or revenue productivity metrics will be able to be established to monitor the return from that investment.

- Secondary measures of program success include training statistics, ideas generated, minutes saved, improved SLAs, reduced late or regulatory penalties, and significant change in the importance and commitment to productivity in internal surveys.

NEUROSCIENCE BEHIND IMPLEMENTATION

In order to form habits and create new neural pathways, there are two primary requirements – attention and positive feedback to that new connection. Attention required is both quality and quantity of attention – called attention density. Ideally, if you would like people to do things a different way, you need to pay regular attention to the small changes initially in order to build on that and create a new habit. Often managers don't praise a beginning or a newly formed skill as the behaviour is only part way to a high-performance habit, but that is precisely when we need to pay attention to and praise that new behaviour.

The positive feedback required can be in the form of a comment such as 'Well done for trying x' or 'That is a great start towards...' or 'Now that you have started that new habit, which is great, how can you practice it on a more frequent basis?'

The combination of attention and positive feedback could be summarised as 'Mind the GAP' – be Mindful of the habit and what is occurring for the person (i.e., the resistance they are overcoming, or fear of getting it wrong), then focus on the Goal (what outcome you are after and help remind the person of this outcome), then pay Attention regularly, quality and quantity, daily or more depending on , the task , and provide Positive feedback often in various forms to the new behaviour, even for small changes or increments or in fact for trying.[29]

An example

At a Monday morning team leaders meeting, Jane leads off by asking about the team's key insights and recommendations from last week's focus on reviewing policy and procedures in relation to customer feedback and complaints. Each team leader had been assigned this task for their specific area. The room was eerily quiet. No one was game to start.

'OK. Let me rephrase my question. How many of you conducted the review?'

'My team had a go, but with everything else going on, I can't say we really did a thorough job', JP, the leader of the accounts team, said. 'We need more time.'

---

29   Kristen Hansen, TRACTION: The Neuroscience of Leadership, enhansenperformance. com.au, 2017.

Mike added, 'We did too. But the same issue. So much going on at the moment, it didn't get the attention I know it deserves given the issues that have arisen over the past quarter.'

'OK. Try this. Say to yourself out loud "silk" five times. Now, spell "silk". What do cows drink?'

As you can imagine we all replied in chorus, 'Milk'. Is that what you thought?

Jane went on to explain that our brains evolved to conserve energy. One of the ways the brain achieves this is turning anything that we do repetitively into a habit. This is very useful, but also has its limitations, as you might have just experienced. Cows drink water!

'Familiarity gives you a sense of security', Jane continued. 'We repeat the same old patterns because we know ahead of time what will happen; we can anticipate the result. The same can't be said for new patterns, where the results we get may be more unpredictable, unreliable and unsettling. OK. Let's try again. What do you put into a toaster?'

Jeff and Mike blurted out 'Toast' and the team broke out in laughter, even though a few of them had said the same thing, albeit much more quietly.

'The problem is that these old patterns become "just good enough" – and trying something different (even if it may be better) can have short-term costs and growth pains that we aren't willing to pay for. Normally, people put bread in a toaster, and take toast out of it. OK. Let me give you all a chance to redeem yourselves … you have to read and answer this one out loud, very quickly. Ready?' Pressing the data projector remote in her hand revealed the following slide:

If a red house is made with red bricks, a blue house is made with blue bricks, a pink house is made with pink bricks, a black house is made with black bricks, what is a greenhouse made with?

This time there was a delay as the group cautiously read the text on the screen, knowing Jane was being tricky. (If you were an observer, you would recognise genuine deliberate effort and see individuals' eyes move up and left to right as they searched for the right answer.) 'Glass!' was the consensus.

Jane continued, 'So what happened in your mind?'

This time there was a delay as the group cautiously read the text on the screen, knowing Jane was being tricky. (If you were an observer, you would recognise genuine deliberate effort and see individuals' eyes move up and left to right as they searched for the right answer.) 'Glass!' was the consensus.

Jane continued, 'So what happened in your mind?'

Mike chipped in, 'This time I picked up the pattern and slowed down so I could stop my automatic response. I paused and resisted the urge (self-regulation) to blurt out "green bricks".'

'Very good,' Jane replied. 'How many of you moved into a conscious or reflective rather than reflexive or automatic state, and in the process were able to access the correct answer from memory? Well, I hope you did. If not, hopefully a revealing lesson. Anticipation, by the way, is another feature of the brain. Part of the pull of music is that we can anticipate what is coming up when we hear a well-known song. The anticipation of what's coming releases the neurotransmitter dopamine, the pleasure hormone, into your system and we experience this as a reward. Its effects don't last long, but, hey, another line of the song continues and our brains recognise what's coming – another little hit of pleasure.'

Jane asks for a volunteer and Jeff, keen to make amends for his recent performance, steps forward. Jane takes a bit of lightweight thread and ties it once around his wrists. She tells the group, 'This string represents the power of doing something one time. Can you break the string?' Jeff easily breaks the thread with a small flick of his wrists. Jane smiles while wrapping the string around the Jeff's wrists many times and repeats the challenge to break it. Despite repeated efforts, the lightweight thread is too strong for Jeff.

'Now you see the power of repeated actions...habits. It takes more than mere willpower and personal strength to break them. It takes a change in the way you think about the problem. Some habits are extremely useful and remain relevant, such as being able to drive a manual gearshift, or climbing a set of stairs. Habits that were highly relevant when they were created, say when you were five years old, may still be running, even though they are no longer the best way of achieving the purpose – the brain "sets it, and forgets it".'

THE CONSCIOUS BRAIN OR PREFRONTAL CORTEX (PFC)

The conscious brain, known as the prefrontal cortex (PFC) is where we pay attention, think, plan, inhibit, and decide. It relies on short-term or working memory, which is part of the PFC. This is known as the reflective system or System 2.

Try to complete the following exercise without using a calculator. You are driving a bus from Sydney to Newcastle. In Sydney, 17 people get on the bus. In North Sydney, six people get off the bus and nine people get on. In St Leonards, two people get off and four get on. In Chatswood, 11 people get off and 16 people get on. In Pymble, three people get off and five people get on. In Gosford, six people get off and three get on. You then arrive at Newcastle. Now, what was the name of the bus driver? Think about it some more. Was the driver's name mentioned? The answer is no.

The PFC has very limited capacity. It can only process between one and three things at any one time.

THE NON-CONSCIOUS BRAIN

When we are using our reflexive system, we exert minimal effort and have massive capacity. It is hard to distract it and it allows us to walk and chew gum at the same time, whilst ensuring that our heart is pumping blood, our food is being digested and a host of other operations are occurring to keep us safe and alive. The brain has evolved to automate as much as it can, so that we don't need to think about how to put on our shoes each morning or how to clean our teeth.

Want to test this? Returning to the team meeting, Jane asks the team to bring their hands together to intertwine their fingers. Jane demonstrated and the group followed. 'Which thumb is on top? Do it three more times and now try to ensure that the other thumb is on top. What happened? Was it more difficult, awkward and cumbersome. Did you have to think about it?'

'I reckon this is why leading and managing change, and breaking habits, can be so hard,' Mark said.

'You're right, Mark, and knowing your brain allows you to train your brain in order to make the changes you need to be more of what you can be,' Jane added. 'Dave, you want to add something?'

'Thanks. A few years ago I injured myself at a Bikram Yoga class. It was my fourth class and I was attempting to copy the cute woman in front of me, who was significantly more advanced and elegant at the posture we were being encouraged to adopt than I was. The end result, I found I couldn't move my left arm. It was as if the upper left side of my body was paralysed and I was in intense pain. After x-rays and an MRI scan, it seemed I had aggravated a nerve in my neck which resulted in "frozen" shoulder. I hope none of you have had the experience of frozen shoulder, because it is bloody painful, debilitating and lasts for anything from five months to a number of years. My doctor said it sometimes appears, particularly in women, without any particular known cause.

'As a result of this frozen shoulder, when it came to putting on a jacket, or shirt, I had to change which arm went in first. Whenever I wasn't thinking, and was on automatic pilot (using the reflexive system, I got feedback very rapidly – pain!) So, I kept correcting, until now, years later, I am still doing it this way. I developed a new habit. The feedback, in terms of physical pain, was actually useful. I was motivated to minimise the pain by using the other arm, in my case my left. The trouble is, when there is no immediate feedback, you are just as likely to keep doing what comes "naturally" even if this is what you want to change.'

Jane added, 'Thank you, Dave. Has the shoulder recovered fully?'

'Thankfully, yes.'

Jane continued, 'My coach was telling me last week that the reflexive system is super-efficient and thus conserves our energy. By comparison, our reflective system, the PFC, requires us to pay attention, think, compare choices and decide. This is heavy work by comparison to the reflexive, automatic system, and consumes considerable resources, i.e. oxygen, sugar (glucose) and dopamine. He said the latest research indicates that our capacity for quality thinking, problem-solving and decision-making, using the conscious reflective system, is very limited. It recommends we do such work when we are fresh and can give it our full attention. He suggested I read Nobel prize winner Daniel Kahneman's book, *Thinking, Fast and Slow*.

'So,' Jane asked, 'what can we do to ensure we get the best from the limited capacity of our PFC?'

'Keep eating and drinking?' Mike half-jokingly suggested, which brought a laugh from the group.

It can be very difficult to get rid of old habits. Habits are well-formed brain circuitry or neural maps, that are created when brain cells (neurons) repeatedly fire together. 'Neuron's that fire together, wire together' is a well-known saying in neuroscience. We are learning now that it appears to be more efficient and effective to create new neural maps rather than trying to change, or dig out, the old ones. In other words, in terms of practical application, don't worry about an old habit you want to change, for example using the word 'but' (which can be seen as dismissive of what someone has just said), rather focus on creating a new habit, replacing it with the word 'and'.

In our garden we have some areas that are tiled. Some of the tiles had become uneven due to the spreading roots of a nearby tree. Having removed the tiles I began digging out these roots. I would take hold of a thinner root with both hands, and by pulling hard reveal where it was heading and where it had come from. At the surface I could sometimes pull out a good section of it, and in the process reveal further webs of roots that were holding it in place. As I continued, I was staggered by the complexity of the root system with its weaving and matting. No wonder the tree was able to resist and withstand high winds.

When you look at the different types of neurons in the brain, they can look much like a variety of trees and their root systems. This is reflected in some of the terms used when referring to brain development such as arborisation and pruning of neurons. Part of a neuron, the axon, can be pruned as part of normal development and this process plays a key role in learning and memory. Another important process, apoptosis — the purposeful death of an entire cell — is also crucial because it allows the body to cull broken or incorrectly placed neurons. But both processes have been linked with disease when improperly regulated

HOW DO WE CREATE NEW HABITS?

'The act of repeatedly paying attention to something (observing) appears to keep the brain circuitry associated with what is being observed stable, so that new mental maps/brain circuitry can be created.'[30] By intentionally choosing where to put your focus, you can play a significant role in changing the structure and function of your own brain, you mind, and your capacity to effectively lead and optimally perform. This takes mental effort, high levels of self-awareness and self-regulation, and knowing that the brain and mind are interwoven.

> 'Habit is a cable;
> we weave a thread of it every day,
> and at last we cannot break it.'

So wrote Horace Mann (1796–1859), an American educator considered to be the father of American education.

The electrochemical exchange between neurons, which occurs at the synapse, is predominantly decided at a non-conscious level outside of our awareness. The impact of this is profound. This means that our brains are being constructed in a way that may not be in line with what we consciously intend for ourselves, which is why the reality we experience sometimes doesn't match up with the outcome we had hoped for.

Think of practising a skill such as a golf swing. If you keep repeating the swing incorrectly, you are wiring the brain to be able to reproduce this, automatically as a habit. That's why having a coach can be so important, because you need the feedback to correct. Using the concepts, models and habits in this book correctly is vital.

---

30   H. Stapp, J.M. Schwartz & M. Beauregard, *Quantum theory in neuroscience and psychology: A neurophysical model of mind-brain interaction*, Philosophical Transactions of the Royal Society of London, 2005.

Therefore when presented with a familiar situation, we are likely to respond habitually/reflexively. Daniel Kahneman describes this as System 1, the automatic, reflexive system, which is our comfort zone. We don't have to think, we just do what we have always done, non-consciously.

Implications – a person new to a supervisory or management role will respond to stressful situations that arise in their habitual way, learned from observing role models of leadership, such as their parents, sports coaches, and teachers. These reflexive responses may not be the most appropriate for the present situation, but can be tough to suppress, or change.

By contrast new wiring appears to be easy to create, and the deeper this new path becomes, the more the old path is not used and is replaced by the new behaviour. This new behaviour eventually becomes the dominant one through the process of paying attention, repetition and positive reinforcement. Eventually, you no longer need to pay attention as the behaviour has become automatic – a habit and an integral part of the reflexive system.

CHAPTER TAKEAWAYS

- The five main themes:

1. Employees need to feel empowered and in control of what they do every day, and management needs to listen, too

2. Leaders model and reinforce 4+1 Habits – senior leaders walk the talk

3. A balance between standardisation and customisation is necessary to maximise engagement

4. The use of a Productivity Maturity Assessment Grid provides teams with the ability to gauge increasing progress for each of the 4+1 Habits

- Plus 1

5. **Use local champions skilled in the habits for immediate reinforcement and support**

CHAPTER 4

EMBEDDING
THE HABITS

A habit is hard to give up. Recall that employee habits are the 'muscle memory' of an organisation, and it is the collective sum of such habits repeated day in and day out across an organisation that naturally sustains, and even accelerates an organisation's ability to deliver! Repeated day after day with little thought or reflection, habits are a deep-rooted network of routines and behaviours. Good habits and behaviours generally lead to good outcomes, just as bad habits and routines can lead to bad outcomes. Trying to improve performance outcomes means making employees stronger by building muscle memory through the introduction and implementation of good behaviours and routines.

The previous chapter stressed the introduction, implementation, and sustainability of a program built around the 4+1 Habits that begins with a collective desire to change, includes a robust implementation plan, and logical alignment to organisational goals and objectives. Ownership is also a key ingredient, with adequate time to personalise and integrate new routines into daily and weekly rhythms, as well as personalised VMBs and SOPs to match department or team standards. It is important to remember to balance between the need to adhere to any and all corporate standards versus customisation to maximise engagement. Too many standards can stifle organisational creativity and buy-in, but too much freedom makes it difficult to grow consistently and evenly, as well as to share best practices.

However, as previously mentioned, even habits need help...it can't be all 'carrot'. Sometimes, a little 'stick' can help sustain a new program. The idea of a team accreditation to recognise, assess, and continually improve an entire organisation's 4+1 Habits program has been shown to be essential in the ongoing commitment and operability. This can be achieved as follows.

- Recognition – Recognise teams that have achieved significant business maturity and capability using 4+1 Habits, basic quality tools, and performance benefits

- Evidence of using 4+1 in daily routines – Gauge the frequency of use and the ownership level across teams

- Participation – Engage middle managers in the early phases of adoption before spreading to more departmental or cross-site engagements

- Increasing program requirements – Seek evidence of team-based process improvements, quantifiable service and efficiency improvements, training levels, and participation in green belt or other certification programs

- Continuous improvement – Provide teams with a self-assessment report to identify usage, consistency, and the basis for an action plan to bridge any gap to make further progress in team maturity.

- Maturity assessment – Allow teams and the organisation to compare and track capability (scale of 1–5) across all five habits using a maturity assessment grid for each of the 4+1 Habits

As discussed earlier accreditation programs can take on a Bronze, Silver or Gold motif to track the progress of teams as they develop further capability and deliver information to the continuous learning of the organisation:

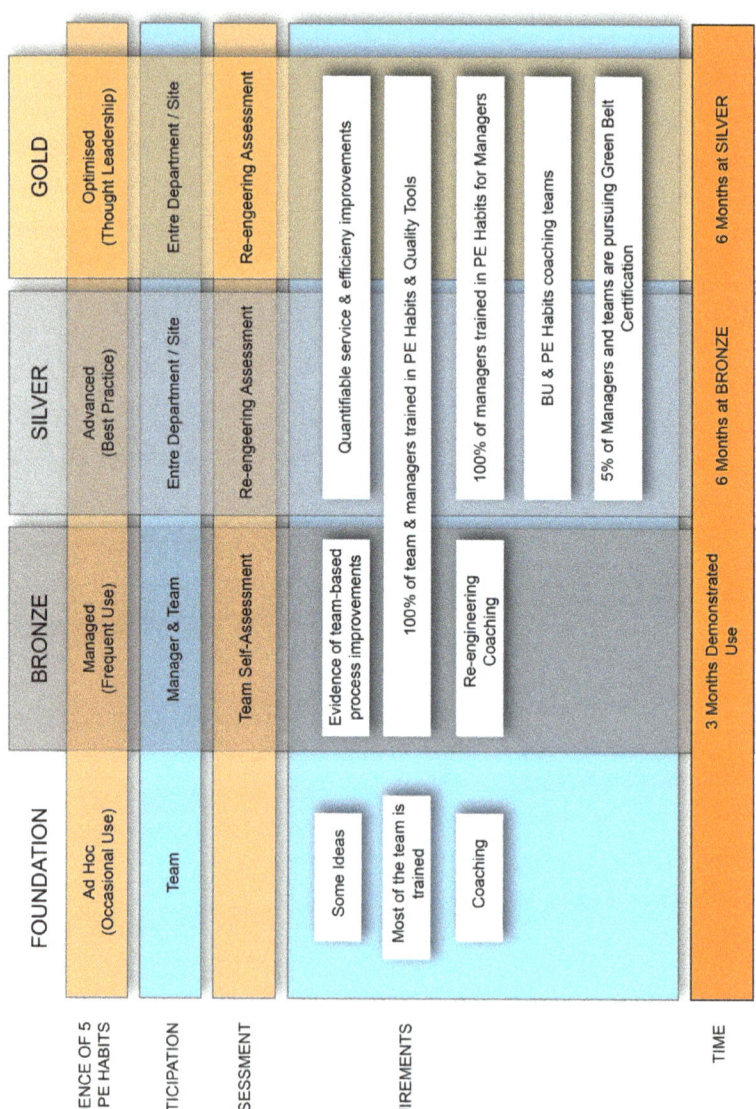

Figure 4.1 Cultural maturity pathway

BUILD CAPABILITY THROUGH ACCREDITATION

A team accreditation program initially involves self-assessment of how well a team has adopted a true continuous improvement mindset and is displaying the right behaviours:

- Customer focus – Understand the value a team provides to customers, and make decisions based on what the customer needs:

  » Customer(s) known requirements

  » Feedback is used regularly and part of the continuous improvement cycle

  » Customer Value Proposition (CVP) is in place and used to drive decisions and prioritise improvements

  » Measures of customer deliverables are monitored, and the measures evaluated for improvement opportunities

- Productivity capability – Use quality tools because they help a team get better outcomes by adding more value, prioritising effectively, and creating tangible benefits:

  » Team's program is well established and ALL employees participate in frequent huddles

  » Appropriate approach/tools are used for problem solving

  » The entire team participates in training, including the middle manager

  » Continuous improvement benefits are measured

- Process management – Apply end-to-end process thinking and managing process performance using customer-centric metrics:

  » Creation of process maps, including establishing owners and governance

  » Create, use and establish governance of SOPs

  » VMBs are effective, value-adding, and continuously improving

  » Metrics drive action

- Productivity mindsets and behaviours – Know what productivity means and understand the benefits it has brought to customers and employees. Teams consistently apply relevant tools to improve delivery:

  » Huddles are scheduled and well-attended

  » Most team members contribute to continuous improvement

  » Continuous improvement ideas are tracked, and behaviours are regularly recognised

  » The entire team develops skills and capabilities

  » Productivity KPIs are in place at all levels

- Productivity leadership – Active champions promote the value of repeatable habits and productivity. Enquiry-based coaching is in place to drive better performance outcomes:

  » Leaders champion the importance of productivity and actively model appropriate leadership behaviour

» Productivity language is the norm

» Coaching is provided at all levels

» All suggestions for improvements are valued and are part of the daily discussion

CONTINUOUS IMPROVEMENT – VMBs

VMBs need a high degree of tender loving care to ensure they remain a true proxy for team performance and engagement, and go a long way in sustaining the 4+1 Habits program across an organisation. The proliferation of VMBs across the organisation give a program acceleration and credibility as employees and managers all want to be a part of a growing trend. VMBs grow with a team, and need to reflect evolving understanding of customer value, metrics, performance against targets, and communication protocols.

But more and more VMBs is not really the answer. VMBs also need consistency and structure to encourage and promote proper team behaviour and interaction:

- CVPs should be referenced at every huddle, and refined as customer needs change. They should describe why the team exists and the unique value it brings. Think about today, but evolve to the future.

- Performance measures should always be challenged and scrutinised as to the sensitivity and correlation to the CVP. Always be looking to move from reactive to proactive, and from discrete to continuous measures as indicators of performance capability. Graphs should always be evolving and raw data (check sheets) should disappear after the first few iterations.

- Continuous Process Improvement (CPI) ideas should be tracked from where they came from, and success regularly celebrated! Small team wins can add up to big morale boosts, and can be tracked on VMBs with considerable ease.

- Actions always need an owner with an agreed due date with regular reference to progress during team huddles.

- Finally, additional information is always part of what personalises every VMB. Let the colour and vibrancy of creative teams shine through without getting out of hand.

CASE STUDY

VALUE OF 4+1 HABITS AT CBA

This case study of a major Australian bank covers a large-scale operation focused on working with retail banking customers. It had a number of sub-teams, multiple internal and external stakeholders and a patchy history of success or failure. This team ended up gaining recognition internally (company's annual productivity and leadership awards) and externally (Shingo Silver Medallion, PEX Award for Culture) for their continuous improvement performance:

- Delivering year on year cost productivity of 10% or more

- Shifting under-performing employee cultures to global best in class

- Improving business outcomes including customer quality by 15% annually and;

- Fostering a watertight operational risk management environment.

The business leaders had to decide how to approach a transformation opportunity where the business itself is highly complex, operates in a very sensitive environment and experiences the typically high staff turnover of any service operations unit.

An additional constraint common to financial services businesses is the high cost of large-scale systems changes and the historical experience of planned deliverables not matching actual outcomes.

While the very top leaders (general manager and senior executives) were brought into these teams from outside the organisation, the remaining executive and senior management teams either remained in place or were filled with existing company employees. These new top leaders were experienced Lean practitioners. At the start, there was some existing awareness of continuous improvement but little practice.

The leadership team therefore focused on two inter-related questions:

- How do we develop a system that changes the way the existing leaders think and also produces sufficient new leaders of the right calibre on an ongoing basis?

- How do we build a self-sustaining culture which meets the holistic business challenges coming up?

Of initial critical importance was crystallising what 'success' looked like and turning that into a compelling vision of the future that everyone (approximately 850 employees in one instance) could understand and get behind. The leaders judged that this would engender the right conditions for a desired optimistic approach to 'change' and start to inspire all employees to want to be a part of the journey.

While acknowledging the continuous nature of ongoing improvement, the leadership team started by using Lean thinking to set a series of time-bound process change goals. Two examples were improving the design and use of technology and resource planning to ensure customer contact occurred only when most convenient for customers;

and removing bottlenecks from lengthy legal processes to provide certainty to customers faster than ever before. It is key to the success of the business units in this case study that functional expertise was combined with solid Lean expertise to conceptualise what 'good' looked like and deliver financial benefits early on.

The next step was to blend these 'hard' changes with an overall sense of purpose aligned with the higher-level company's vision and strategy around customer-centricity. Firstly, each team of roughly 15 people was tasked with creating a Customer Value Proposition taking a lead from the company's vision which could then be synthesised into a True North for the whole business unit. Facilitated sessions then helped the teams 'backwards image' into the future to describe what the customer experience would be like and what the business unit would look like in a few years' time. From there the team developed a set of strategic pillars such as only investing in technology where it supported the True North or focusing on developing a broader range of solutions for customers. A multi-modal communications effort was then devised and rolled out (through workshops, town halls, intranet, huddles etc.) to deliver the coherent plan, seek further input and motivate people to commit themselves to the plan.

The True North and the 'pillars' became a shorthand used by staff within the business as a mirror/sense-check for activities as diverse as holding conversations with customers on the phone to prioritising projects. Similarly, the balance achieved between customer outcomes, shareholder outcomes and community (stakeholder/regulator) outcomes was vital in creating strategic alignment with upstream business units. It created a common bond too, describing shared expected customer-centric behaviours and building informal relationships between staff members.

At the same time as creating the high-level direction of the business and deciding which large-scale changes were going to be made, the executive team knew that a 'license to operate' also depended on churning out good, predictable daily/weekly/monthly results through a strong operating rhythm which would be foundational to the cultural change they sought.

The first step towards this was the introduction of a standard coaching model for all employees across the business. This systematically structured reviews of the different parts of an employee's performance, highlighted options to alter or improve and created a change and review plan between the employee and direct manager. Thus, from Day 1 any new employee was being introduced to the fundamentals of Plan, Do, Check, Act thinking in a concrete, relevant way. Staff were expected to start reviewing performance, think systematically about what had gone well or could change, then trial these changes and review again. This set of behaviours started to become pervasive.

The second big thing the operating rhythm had to do was make smart use of data and be appropriately evaluative of performance – that meant reacting to the right things and ignoring 'noise'. There were two big investments to be made to achieve this: creating a rich management of information (MI) environment providing all the important pieces of performance data for leading and lagging measures on time and in the required levels of granularity; and building the skills in the teams (agent, supervisors and managers) to interpret and respond to the data correctly.

A big investment was made in a DataMart solution that pulled data from all systems (contact systems, workforce planning systems, HR systems, core product systems, etc.) and amalgamating them into a single dataset. This enabled multi-dimensional analysis of data and at any level of granularity. Even more important, arguably, was the presentation of this data via a queriable intranet presentation layer to every single person in the business. Now everyone could see and own the performance of the business and because KPIs were all aligned from bottom to top everyone could see exactly how their actions impacted business outcomes.

Alongside this data investment began the creation of 'scientists of the future', the term the business used to describe the training of both PDCA 'scientific thinking' and statistical, variation-management skills for all employees. This was designed as a 'rolling-refresher' program backed by coaching in performance review meetings or 1-to-1s as part of 'leader's standard work'. Together with the coaching model described above, people now had the data analysis skills to refine and target their PDCA behaviours...continuous improvement had become a habit at all levels.

The business now had a good structure of improved customer and shareholder outcomes in place and a strong operating rhythm. From an initial point where financial targets were routinely missed, the business moved into a phase where it started to outperform on a productivity basis and made significant contributions to the company's bottom line. Similarly, investments in root-cause analysis had seen customer complaints reduce even as the number of customers contacted massively increased. The business even had the beginnings of a talent pipeline with the strong foundation of data-based PDCA thinking all staff received. The leadership team knew from past experience, though, that it was the discretionary effort that members of staff put in that made the difference to sustained performance.

One of the most interesting things about service operations/call centres is the amount of knowledge, training and skills which are latent in the workforce and rarely get tapped. Talking to customers on the phone all day are maths and economics graduates, communications specialists, graphic artists, musicians, dancers etc. Being able to unleash some of this latency not only makes work a more fulfilling place for people to come to but also boosts the sorts of things businesses can do.

The business therefore created a whole raft of tiered staff and leadership development programs and a whole 'wave of talent' initiative that allowing people to perform their own music, create their own videos, write books and create and host town hall events, etc. Structured development courses for new employees, opportunities for creative input into business communications and work events all led directly to better staff engagement, direct customer benefit in terms of improved service or processes, and a stronger sense of shared purpose.

The key by-product of this was that it created opportunities for people to step up, take the initiative and lead things. In doing so, senior leaders were exposed to talented employees and vice versa. A number of potential leaders were identified this way.

Another key outlet for this creativity and discretionary effort, combined with creating a sense of place in the community aligned to the business's True North, was the charity support the team pursued. In addition to the more usual fundraising fun activities, the team was also successful in supporting the charities with skilled volunteering: social media marketing consulting, running projects, communication design and many other proficiencies. One estimate had it that the comparable cost of hiring consultants to do the same work outweighed the cash donations the business made by 6:1.

What has been described so far is the approach to making large-scale changes to key business processes, setting up a data-driven operational rhythm and facilitating a strong staff engagement culture where people are willing to go the extra mile. The final piece of the jigsaw for both building a business culture which delivers stretch targets consistently and for creating the leadership cadre of the future is embedding conscious Continuous Improvement practice.

The business leadership team took the approach from the start that CI tools, habits and techniques should be rolled out not as artefacts to be marvelled at and admired for their intrinsic worth but that they should be introduced into people's daily practice as items of utility for tasks they were already performing. They likened the concept to planting seeds in already fertile ground. For example, as staff got into the habit of using performance data to understand what was going on the business, the team introduced visual management boards and team huddles to make this existing practice more productive. Similarly, as the concept of PDCA thinking caught hold through the embedded coaching model then basic CI tools such as Ishikawa diagrams and Lean 8 wastes were rolled out and regular CI/Workout sessions were scheduled in for every team.

 The deliberate plan, based on previous experience, was to introduce tools and ideas which people could practically see working for them and then to give people enough time to generate mastery of these before moving on to other, more complex ones. This is where the 4 core habits played a key role. Rather than train 100 people in the use of 10 tools, and see only some people master them all, the strategy was to roll out the habits to over 100 people and see everyone learn to use them well.

With each of these roll-outs came the message from the leadership team that the sustainability of the business improvement journey depended on lots of small changes that each team could make and not the only the big ones that had historically got the whole thing off the ground. Employees were now accountable for reviewing performance, listening to the voice of the customer and finding better ways to work. Everyone in the business shared expectations around data-based decision making and 'test and learn' behaviours. This was reinforced with an internal CI awards scheme (with meaningful rewards) and regular nominations for the higher-level company recognition program.

There were some amazing results from this team-based problem solving including a 90% improvement in customer quality for one key regulated process, massive reductions in inter-operator variation and fixes to issues with customer data that no-one had previously known existed. And, of course, it was another opportunity for talented employees to learn this way of thinking, demonstrate an ability to make a difference and join the talent pipeline.

The journey continues now with two areas of focus; improving in-depth knowledge of the link between continuous improvement (Shingo) principles and practices for all employees and rolling out advanced training in Lean projects for managers and supervisors. As always, the leadership team are ensuring people have a profound appreciation for the practical value of CI in their daily lives before delivering more complex or abstract concepts.[31]

NEUROSCIENCE BEHIND THE HABITS AND MINDFULNESS

In a study conducted by Ellen Langer, Timothy Russell and Noah Eisenkraft, and Noah Eisenkraft,[32] orchestra musicians were instructed to be either mindless or mindful. In this case, being mindless meant replicating a previous performance with which they were very satisfied. The mindful instructions directed them to make the piece new in very subtle ways that only they would know. (They were playing classical music and not jazz, so the novel distinctions were indeed subtle.) The authors reported, 'Their performance was recorded and then played for audiences unaware of our instructions. We found that not only did the musicians much prefer playing mindfully, the mindfully played pieces were judged as superior. Everyone was in a sense mindfully doing their own thing and the result was a better co-ordinated outcome.'

---

31   Interview with Jon Pratlett, 11 January 2017, www.JonPratlett.com
32   Ellen Langer, Timothy Russell & Noah Eisenkraft, 'Orchestral performance and the footprint of mindfulness', *Psychology of Music*, Vol. 37, No. 2, 2009.

CHAPTER TAKEAWAYS

- The four main themes

1. People understand how the Habits link together

2. People understand the why the Habits drive the right outcomes

3. Linking customers to business outcomes

4. Continuously lifting the expectations of the outcomes of behaviours and habits

- Plus 1

5. **Continuously lifting expectations around habits delivers sustainability**

CHAPTER 5

MATURING THE HABITS

Chapter 2 looked at the habits in general, Chapter 3 was all about how to implement them as a part of an overall program, Chapter 4 is about starting to embed the habits, so it's a logical next step to explore how to continually improve and mature each of the 4+1 habits.

One of the traps to avoid with the habits is to become overly focused on Key Performance Indicators that are likely to drive the wrong behaviour. For example, we could measure how many problem-solving meetings have taken place and give teams a target. The risk is that they will have lots of meetings but not necessarily of the right quality to fix the issues. So instead we suggest the focus should be on Key Behavioural Indicators (KBIs) which aim to drive and support the right behaviours needed to embed the habits. KBIs can be tricky to develop and there is no easy off-the-shelf list. Indeed, many people feel uncomfortable with the concept because KBIs can often seem much less tangible than a KPI and need a lot of experimentation and regular change if they are to be useful. Another reason organisations are often uncomfortable with KBIs is that they are usually not something that can be defined at the executive level and cascaded down through the organisation. Indeed it may be useful to give the individual teams the opportunity to try and develop their own KBIs and experiment to see what works. To stimulate thinking we have included a few examples of potential KBIs for each habit in the advanced sections of this chapter. We are not suggesting these are the best or only KBIs – the examples are intended to illustrate the concept. We encourage teams to have a go at defining their own, monitor the results and keep experimenting.

CONTINUOUSLY IMPROVING AND MATURING VMBS

Scale	Basic			Intermediate	Advanced
	1	**2**	**3**	**4**	**5**
Visual Management Boards	There are no visual displays such as posted metrics, performance metrics etc	Visual displays exist, but are often not regularly updated or used effectively to take action	Visual displays are understood and track meaningful performance indicators. Trigger points that require intervention are set for formal corrective action	Visual displays are implemented and maintained by teams. The displays are the primary tool for communication of current status, planning & evaluating performance	Every aspect of the performance measures, KPI, action items, KBI, and meetings are displayed in the team area under standard formats designed by the team

Figure 5.1 Maturing Visual Management Boards

Summarising VMBs from Chapter 2:

- The VMB is at the heart of the habits, providing a focal point for teams to review performance, set priorities, solve problems and manage continuous improvement activities.

- It is both a tool (i.e., a visual management board) and a habit (i.e., the use of the VMB as it is continuously updated with performance data, progress on CI activities, team specifics, and customer experiences).

The VMB tells the team's story:

- Customer Value Proposition (CVP): clearly defines why the team exists and the unique value it delivers to the customer (links True North and customer value);

- Performance Measures: select key measures that give a rounded view of the team's process(es), including quality, efficiency, customer satisfaction, and risk. It uses a mixture of historic (taillight) and forward (headlight) data to highlight disconnects between output and targets. Just as a picture paints a thousand words, so does a good graph!

- Continuous Process Improvement (CPI): tracks improvement ideas and completions and helps to celebrate success.

- Actions: there is always an owner to every action with agreed-to dates and visibly displayed progress.

- Additional information: every team is different and chooses to use their boards to best meet their needs. If the team feels they own their VMB, they will use their VMB!

It's very important to remember that a good VMB evolves and grows with a team. As the team learns more, and begins to change the way it thinks and acts, the VMB should naturally follow. Just as with any new endeavour, it's counter-productive to expect perfection on the first go. Using a VMB should never be an administrative burden, rather it should become a touchstone for the team. A place where the team comes 'to see'. Very much Go Gemba, the team (and others) comes to the VMB to learn, listen and grow. Don't be intimidated by other teams. Leverage from what you see, adopt best practices, and quickly disregard what no longer works.

There are generally three levels of VMB maturity, as shown in Figure 3.1, The productivity maturity assessment grid.

- **BEGINNER** (levels 1, 2 and 3) – the team is learning to develop how to visually display what they do and how they deliver to a customer. It's early days ... and still not part of the daily rhythm of the team. The CVP is in constant revision. The metrics tend to be discrete, historic and not directly related to customer outcome. Generally, the team's manager 'owns' the board as the sole contributor.

- **INTERMEDIATE** (level 4) – the VMB has been up and running 6 months and is beginning to use more continuous and forward-looking output measures to better gauge output relative to customer expectations and targets. The VMB is a focus for the team. The team is continually flexing and adapting new lessons into the VMB and the way the team interfaces and reacts. Ownership is more distributed with several team members contributing to daily content. Data drives action.

- **ADVANCED** (level 5) – the board has become an inseparable part of the rhythm and team dynamics. Metrics are near real-time with direct correlation and relevance to customer satisfaction. There is a consistency and simple logic to the entire board (i.e. any gaps in customer delivery have an exact link to CPI and actions). Any visitor could easily interpret what's going on and understand the team's 'story'.

Let's listen to a coach discuss each of these separately as it relates to the VMB

BEGINNER VMB MATURITY (LEVELS 1, 2 AND 3)

Customer Value Proposition

Team purpose or CVP is tricky to get right. It's either too lofty, too wordy, or lacks sufficient detail. Teams usually start off on what they do and require some prompting or coaching to crystallise their thoughts. Here is an example of a debt collection/account receivable team coaching session around the initial CVP:

- Coach: 'What value do we add to the customer?'

- Team: 'We get customers to pay their arrears asap!'

- Coach: 'How do you currently measure this?'

- Team: 'Time to payment, closing arrears, or for secured loans, debt recovered.'

- Coach: 'Taking a customer centric view ... how does the customer feel when they get called?'

- Team: 'We are a collections team, so naturally they are embarrassed and ashamed when we call and don't want to talk to us.'

- Coach: 'Do you think a customer would like to know that you are measuring their interaction with you using metrics like "time to pay" and "closing arrears". Seems rather internally focused, wouldn't you think?'

- Team: 'True, but we're a business and they should expect that.'

- Coach: 'How would you want them to feel?'

- Team: 'Respected. We want them to feel like we calling to help them get back on track'

- Coach: 'Wonderful! You want them to understand why they are behind, and that you are calling to help. So, let's think about what real value you add to the customer and how you can help them get back on track and feel respected.'

- Coach: 'Re-think about the value you add to the customer.'

- Team: 'We understand their position and can work with them to come up with a solution that gets them closer to reducing if not eliminating the arrears in a short or reasonable time frame!'

- Coach: 'Good. Make it tighter. Shorten it. Focus!'

- Team: 'We respectfully help customers return to a better financial position.'

- Coach: 'How does that feel for a team Customer Value Proposition or Team Purpose?'

- Team: 'Really good.'

- Coach: 'Yes, it's a good start. With a great purpose, how could you measure that you were meeting this and meeting the business metrics you have?'

Metrics

So now let's explore developing measures for success in both meeting this CVP and the business needs:

- The coach left us with the question: '... how could you measure that you were meeting this and meeting the business metrics you have?'

- 'Start with your current team KPIs (Key Performance Indicators)'

- 'How do they align to the new CVP?'

With metrics, it is important to just start measuring something! Even if it is the number of customers committing to make a payment on their arrears. A simple measure that is a single point for the previous day or previous week is fine; just putting something up on the board will start better conversations in the team. Once the team start completing the daily metric for a while, then they should ask the question as to what is a good or realistic target that the team should be aiming for in an outbound debt recovery call centre.

For example

	Mon	Tues	Wed	Thurs	Fri	Target
Average Handling time (s)	124	141	137	161		135

Plotting the daily numbers as a team overall, then also plotting the results for each team member and understanding what was driving their daily result, types or call, i.e. first, follow-up, what is driving the variation in the team etc. Starting off with single point then adding a target is a good one to drive the right conversations. Then, to drive even better conversations, display the data in a time series to understand the level of variation. A simple time series plot is good. Here is an example of a coaching conversation.

- Coach: 'How do you feel about missing/exceeding the target?'

- Team: 'We look at the metrics?'

- Coach: 'What do you need to do to meet the target consistently or what did you do to exceed the target that you could do more of?'

- Team: 'We need to understand what is causing the variation from target and then establish the root cause.'

- Coach: 'What can we learn from person x on exceeding the target?'

- Team: 'We could understand what they do and potentially copy that so others can learn.'

- Coach: 'What can we do as a team to help person y meet target?'

- Team: 'Ideally coach them, or buddy them up.'

Team check-in

We all bring our everyday emotions with us into work, so it's good to get an upfront feel for the team right from the start. This is easily done by starting the huddle in front of the VMB and asking each assembled team member how they feel on a simple score out of 10, 0 being terrible (and I should not be here) through to 9 or 10 (feeling fantastic). It is important the team feels safe and understands that it is ok to be 5 or 6, because we are human and sometimes things challenge us internally and externally. We may be dealing with disappointment or challenges and that is OK. Another option is to use an x~y matrix on how am I feeling against my workload, with team members putting pictures or magnetic buttons to represent where they are. A frown, neutral, or smiley face on the VMB indicates the overall team emotion. Easy and fun!

Figure 5.2 Team check-in matrix

Team CI

It is important that the team not only highlights opportunities for continuous improvement (see later in this chapter on huddles), but also sees that it is making progress. This can be done through using a basic system of simply showing which CIs the team are working on and their progress through the PCDA cycle.

It is also helpful for the team to check in with the team on a completed CI. How is that showing up in the current set of metrics? How will the team measure the success of that CI initiative?

INTERMEDIATE VMB MATURITY (LEVEL 4)

Initially review the team CVP. Does it still resonate with the team and have they validated it with their customers, whether internal or external to the organisation.

111

Since the VMB has been running for a few months at this point, it's natural to see that, instead of just focusing on running a few data points against a target, the next step is to plot these KPIs in the form of a time series or run chart.

Here is an example of the Average Handling Time (AHT) for the team shown as a run chart.

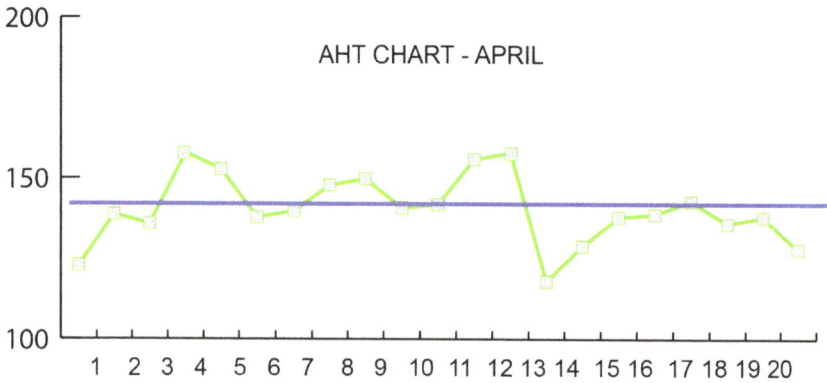

Figure 5.3 Average Handling Time data run chart

Then the coaching questions will centre around what is driving the variation around the target (blue line), and what they could do to reduce variation.

Here is an example of the coaching conversation:

- Coach: 'What trends in variation you are seeing in your metrics?'

- Team: 'We are starting to focus on reducing the variation.'

- Coach: 'How did you decide on your target?'

- Team: 'My boss initially decided, then we went and spoke to our customers.'

- Coach: 'That's great, how are things different from managing on single point data?'

- Team: 'We focus on reducing variation rather than reacting to single point data and now engage with our customer to understand what their expectation is and try also to manage them.'

ADVANCED VMB MATURITY

Moving to the advanced level of the VMB, one would expect more statistical bias and forward-looking (predictive) measures e.g. through a control chart:

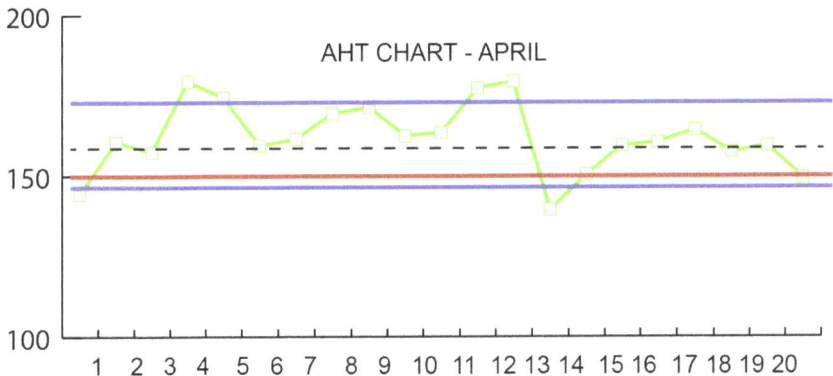

Figure 5.4 Average Handling Time data in a control chart

This shows that the target line is much lower than the team's average performance. This may be an opportunity either to reset the target (although this does have budget/resourcing implications) or it will require a change in the process to move the team performance average to meet the target. This may be possible through PDCA or may require external help from the team.

Greater analysis of the metric could show up in the form of a bar chart or potentially a Pareto chart of constituent parts of the metric to drive the conversations in the huddles.

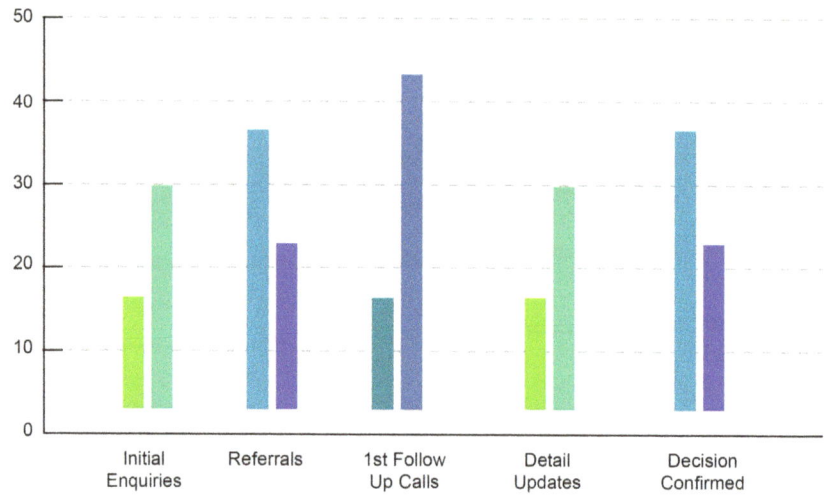

Figure 5.5 Bar chart of reasons for calls

Also at the advanced level, there is a simple rule to test whether the VMB is advanced and that is the '**1-3-10 Test**'.

- Within 1 second an observer walking up to the VMB would know if the team is winning or not.

- Within 3 seconds the observer knows where the team is/is not winning.

- Within 10 seconds the observer can see what actions are being taken in areas where the team is not winning, i.e. restoring their metrics back to on or above target.

On an advanced VMB, not only would you be looking at output KPIs as trends but it becomes very important to measure the inputs or leading indicators that drive that output. A common metric in customer satisfaction and a business metric in call centres is AHT – Average Handling Time. Teams tend to track these KPIs on the VMBs as these are important and often form part of the team's KPI and that of their manager. Customer satisfaction is not how long you are on the phone

– that is a business metric. More important to the customer is whether his or her question was resolved initially, or was the customer handed over to another department to resolve the problem.

Let's look at a typical coaching conversation in around a mature VMB.

- Coach: 'How do you know if the variation you are seeing is due specific changes or just general variation?' With those who have a statistics background, you could ask 'Is this special or common cause variation?'

- Team: 'We could use a control chart to help us.'

- Coach: 'How would you detect a trend before it fails?'

- Team: 'We could use the Westinghouse rules and the upper and lower control limits.'

- Coach: 'How would you know if your improvements are making a material difference to your team's performance?'

- Team: 'We could look at when we implemented each CI and then try to line up an improvement in our metric.'

- Coach: 'How could the team members implementing the change own the improvement?'

- Team: 'Get the team member to draw the line of sight of the CI/PDCA to movement of the metrics.'

- Coach: 'That's great. How would you know that your habits are maturing?'

- Team: 'We could start looking at the draft KBIs we started developing and then refine them over time.'

TYPES OF VMB

The team's function will determine the type and layout of their VMB. For example, if the team is a transactional team that follows repeatable processes producing similar outputs or outcome there will be different VMBs. Examples of types of VMBs are:

- Agile Team VMBs

- Project Team VMBs

KEY BEHAVIOURAL INDICATORS

Here are some examples of KBIs for VMBs:

- A red or green sticker determined by the internal customer(s) who is invited to review the VMB and judge whether it is measuring the things they think are important. I saw this in action recently and it was working well, with a different customer each week being asked to review.

- A big 'Thumbs up' on whether the board passes the '1-3-10 Test' or not.

- The number of changes to what has appeared on the board in the last month.

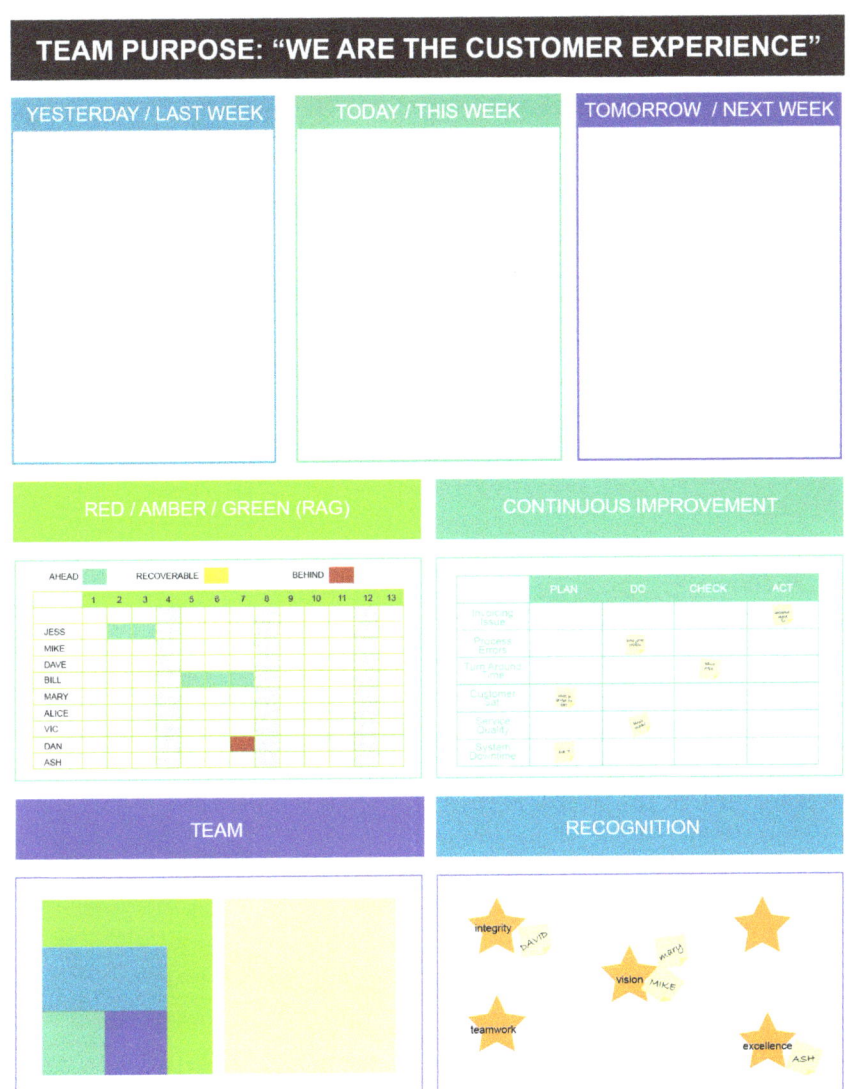

Figure 5.5a Example 1 of VMB layout

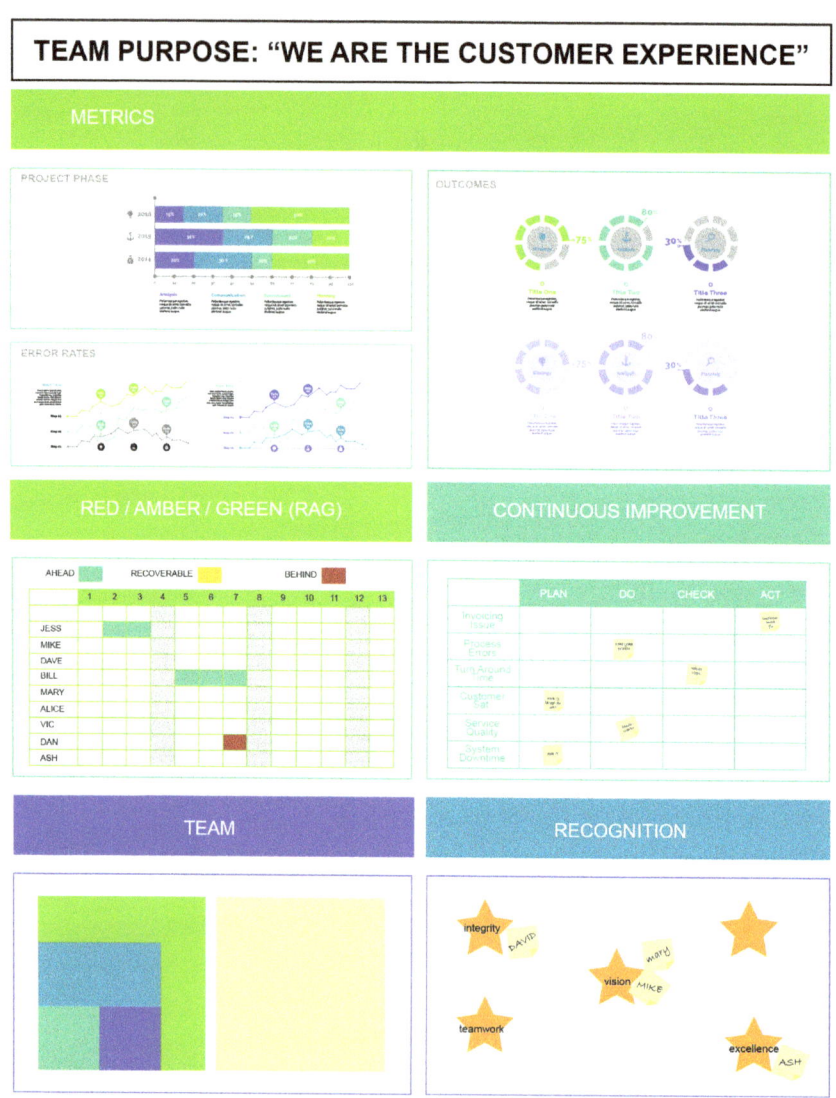

Figure 5.5b Example 2 of VMB layout

VMB TAKEAWAYS

- The four main themes:

1. VMBs are just tools, updating them is the real habit

2. '1-3-10 Test' – Making things visual helps focus the attention of the team on areas to improve

3. Visualising data with colour and targets reduces misunderstandings

4. It's OK to start off at a basic level, then mature the VMB – don't let perfection be the enemy of better.

- Plus 1

5. **I know how to start and mature my VMB**

CONTINUOUSLY IMPROVING AND MATURING HUDDLES

Scale	Basic			Intermediate	Advanced
	1	2	3	4	5
Team Huddles	Not happening anywhere	Sporadic meetings with no set agenda/ structure or timing	Normal daily/ weekly scheduled meetings with set agenda, but agenda does not focus on key segments of VMB	Normal daily/ weekly scheduled meetings with set agenda, huddles carried out around VMB	Daily/weekly meetings occur with set agenda and everyone standing around VMB. Team quickly responds to changing demands

Figure 5.6 Maturing huddles

Think of the VMB as an integral part of the team, helping to tell the team's story. It enhances the quality of the team's conversation by putting the customer at the centre of the story and having the one correct sentence around customer value proposition. EVERYTHING revolves around the team's ability to deliver ever-improving quality to the customer. The huddle is all about communication, action, and accountability:

- Associates or front-line employees regularly update the VMB with real-time information and use the huddle to share how the team is delivering.

- Managers ensure that the 'what' is clear and regularly confirmed in the huddle with the team having a clear understanding of purpose and CVP.

- The frequency and timing are determined by the operating rhythm of the team but should not be less than weekly.

- The duration of the huddle is always fixed and typically takes a maximum of 15 minutes.

- Everyone has their own style, so rather than make the standard practice overly regimented it is better to agree on a few simple principles and behaviours.

A good huddle should:

- Be short and focused

- Review recent performance against targets

- Agree on priorities

- Record actions with clear owners and dates on the board

- Be facilitated by different members of the team

- Be scheduled and take place on a fixed time and day

- Be sequenced to the operating rhythm of the team

Example behaviours

- Associates – Contribute proactively to the huddle discussion.

- Managers – Regularly attend huddles to listen, learn and support the team.

- Leaders – Frequently demonstrate that the huddles are important by role-modelling and by visiting others and asking about them.

BASIC HUDDLES (LEVELS 1 AND 2)

The key to huddles is creating a safe environment. To start off, the leader or even the coach could role-model the huddle, ensuring that people are resolved about the purpose and follow a systematic sequence in discussing the visual board. Let's look at the coaching conversation of the leader and the coach to set up the first huddle.

- Coach: 'What is the purpose of the huddle?'

- Leader: 'We want to have the right conversations?'

- Coach: 'What are the right conversations?'

- Leader: 'Our performance for the customer?'

- Coach: 'How does the VMB help this?'

- Leader: 'It has the metrics.'

- Coach: 'How are you going to make it safe for the team to discuss performance?'

- Leader: 'They are a team, that's not a problem.'

- Coach: 'OK, how can we get the team to express how they are feeling?'

- Leader: 'There is that chart on the VMB.'

- Coach: 'How could you start the conversation to make it safe for others to say that they feel a bit stressed etc.?'

- Leader: 'Oh, that's easy, I could be honest and tell them how I am feeling, being a bit vulnerable but make sure it ends on a positive.'

- Coach: 'What support do you need from me to run your first huddle?'

- Leader: 'Watch me and give me feedback and highlight anything amiss.'

Sometimes it is hard for a leader to lead rather than tell people what to do. Developing this ability is often the start of extending the leader's coaching abilities to the next level. Once the leader has managed to establish the rhythm of running the huddles with all team members beginning to participate, it's time to take the huddle to the next level of maturity.

INTERMEDIATE HUDDLES (LEVELS 3 AND 4)

A key element with huddles is creating a safe environment. To start off, the leader or even the coach could role-model the huddle, ensuring that the team is strict about the purpose and follows a systematic sequence in discussing the visual board. Let's look at the coaching conversation of the leader and the coach to set up the first huddle.

- Coach: 'What is the purpose of the huddle?'

- Leader: 'We want to have the right conversations?'

- Coach: 'What are the right conversations?'

- Leader: 'Our performance for the customer?'

ADVANCED HUDDLES

As the team start to own and mature their huddles the team will want to drive the right conversations in the huddles to identify opportunities for improvement or where it needs to focus or adjust effort because of leading and lagging measures. Here is a guideline to consider what makes a great huddle:

- Check on how everyone is feeling.

- What have you achieved, since we last spoke?

- What are you planning to focus on until our next huddle?

- Any blockers? Any place where you require the Team Leader's assistance?

- Do not run the huddle like a meeting. Keep the conversation moving.

- Have fun.

- Discuss team KPIs (performance).

- What we have done well? What have we not done well?

- Discuss as a group whether we have been on track to our objectives.

- And if there is a need to steer in a different direction and if a problem-solving session is required, assign an action and an owner to pencil in a problem-solving session.

- Team members should discuss continuous improvement opportunities that they would have identified. Quickly share.

- Celebrate success.

Here is a typical coaching conversation:

- Coach: 'The huddles are effective?'

- Team: 'They are getting better, and we try to make them better by trying various team suggestions.'

- Coach: 'What improvements have you made to mature your huddles?'

- Team: 'We have each team member take turns at running the huddle and we have now instigated a finishing question to all team members and visitors, "what can we do to make the huddle better?"'

- Coach: 'Have you had customers/visitors to attend your huddles and what feedback have you received from them?'

- Team: 'Yes, it was a bit scary in the beginning that our customers could see that we were not perfect, but they came up with some great suggestion including having a tiered target for our metrics. They liked hearing about the CIs the team has implemented to make a better experience for customers and staff, and one volunteered to join the PDCA.'

- Coach: 'Have you visited any of your supplier's huddles and offered improvement ideas?'

- Team: 'Like our customers visiting our huddles, we first started with our Team Leader attending our suppliers' huddle. Then, as we got more comfortable, we took turns and it was a great learning to be able to give feedback on the most important things that were affecting us with our suppliers.'

Applying a variation of the 4 questions discussed in Chapter 1, a question in a similar vein is 'What went well (today, yesterday)?' and 'What can we do better next time?', both with an obvious follow-up of 'why' to any response, which can then be analysed as part of the CI work and SOP update review . Most often on operational areas in Financial Services the major topic of conversations in huddles is around resourcing, given they chase demand. They should really be a focus of the conversations on resourcing levels to meet current and projected demand.

KEY BEHAVIOURAL INDICATORS

Here are some examples of KBIs for VMBs:

- Green/amber/red or smiley/sad faces to reflect how the team is feeling.

- Bronze, Silver, Gold star agreed by the team at the end of huddle on how they rated the quality of engagement in the huddle.

- A thumbs up/thumbs down (literally a big cut-out thumb) on the team behaviours during the huddle.

- Number of people from other teams that attend our huddle.

HUDDLE TAKEAWAYS

- The four main themes:

1. Huddles drive employee engagement

2. Use real-time and relevant data to drive conversations

3. Focus on variation and what need to be done today to get back on target

4. It's OK to start off basic then mature the huddle

- Plus 1

5. **I've taken the action to decide the one thing I'm personally going to do to start and mature my huddle**

CONTINUOUS IMPROVEMENT THROUGH PDCA

The third habit is continuous improvement (CI). That means striving every day to improve the customer experience while making the process simpler for ourselves and our colleagues. A summary of Chapter 2 on PDCA:

- There is a very strong link between CI, the VMB and huddles to identify opportunities and set priorities.

- Making CI a habit and linking it directly to the VMB ensures greater alignment to business priorities.

- CI operates within a simple framework (Plan, Do, Check, Act) to encourage widespread adoption across all levels. The PDCA cycle keeps things simple and makes it relatively quick and easy to implement a CI idea whilst at the same time ensuring a standard structure is followed.

- Critical aspect of the CI habit is the reward and recognition system for implementation of improvements.

HOW TO MATURE CI

Scale	Basic			Intermediate	Advanced
	1	2	3	4	5
Continuous Improvement	No Continuous Improvement initiatives anywhere	Continuous improvement initiatives triggered, but there is little action taken on submitted suggestions and as a result , low participation	Continuous Improvement activities occur, but they are random and not tied to business or team objectives	Continuous Improvement tools used to identify improvement opportunities, small improvement opportunities identified and implemented	All process improvements are driven by using Continuous Improvement tools, high impacting opportunities identified and tracking of benefits implemented

Figure 5.7 Maturing CI

We are natural problem solvers. Humankind's evolution has depended upon our ability to adapt to changing circumstances and quickly implement solutions that move us forward. 'We all solve problems every day' is a phrase we hear often. Unfortunately, there are often 'too many problems'. The issue is that there is a tendency to react to every issue or opportunity with an immediate answer. Leaders often do this as they are very experienced but also because they wrongly think that this is their job.

Instead we need to foster a culture of structured problem-solving which uses simple tools to ensure we get to the root cause of the problem before jumping in with a solution which is most likely simply to address some of the symptoms. Instead of focusing on the solution leaders need to focus on the system of thinking and behaviour and encourage the use of learning through practical problem-solving tools.

There are several important aspects to consider about how a leader's behaviour will impact the effectiveness of the CI system. Here is an example.

On a visit to a site in Australia one of the authors was taken on a tour of the fifteen or so Visual Management Boards across the business. They all looked very well set out in a standard format and had clear KPIs and a list of projects being worked on. After the third board, something began to look a bit strange. Every KPI and every project was coloured green. At the end of the tour it was noticeable that the only colour on any board was green. Puzzled and a little suspicious of what was going on, the author had a discussion with the associate showing him round.

Let's see how our coach would help the team:

Coach: 'I couldn't help noticing that every measure and every project is colour coded green.'

Team: 'Well, yes, that's right, because everything is on target and there are no issues!'

Coach: 'Amazing! This must be a fantastic place to work!'

Team: 'Well, not really.'

Coach: 'Why? Everything is green and you appear not to have any problems.'

Team: 'That's true, but the boss doesn't like stuff in red. Every time anyone puts something in red it becomes a major drama and people get blamed for stuffing up. So, it's just easier to show it in green and keep him happy!'

So, while on the one hand 'too many problems' is an issue, having no problems at all is probably even worse! The key message is that it's important not simply to introduce a range of tools and expect them to work. They won't work unless there is also a focus on defining the key behaviours needed to support them.

If we look at this in terms of maturity across the three levels, we might typically see the following:

BEGINNER STAGE

The organisation has developed a standard set of tools to approach problem-solving. These could be a wide range of different approaches or ideally a few simple tools. Selected 'specialists' have been trained in these problem-solving tools and the tools are applied to major problems that require facilitation. Most people experience them infrequently as part of a team pulled together to address an issue. In other words, they are recipients of the process rather than skilled practitioners. There are likely to be 'islands of excellence' where individuals that are early adopters or experienced from previous organisations have spread problem-solving tools across their team or department but they are not yet embedded as an organisation standard.

INTERMEDIATE STAGE

At the intermediate stage the organisation has defined the problem-solving tools that work for them and agreed on the standard approach to their application. This is important for several reasons:

- It sets a clear expectation around the approach to solving problems (or assessing opportunities)

- It means that there is a common language across the organisation so that it's easier for team members to work together and cross functionally to work through problems

- As people move around the business through promotion or transfer they work to a common standard

- Using Plan, Do, Check, Act means that everyone can understand how to effectively manage any problems and understand the next step in the process

At this stage the organisation will have established standard templates for tools such as '5 Whys' and fishbones and these will be used throughout the organisation. Leaders will be trained not only in the application of the tools so that they can lead by example but also in how to coach the use of the tools. An example conversation at this level could be:

Team leader: 'We've got this issue with a backlog of claim type x and we just can't keep up with the demand.'

Leader: 'OK, can you talk me through the problem-solving analysis you have done?'

Associate: 'Err. Well, we are really struggling to hit the numbers so we have been too busy to take time out to do that.'

Leader: 'OK, but we need to be able to understand the root cause. What do you think we can do to help us get to this?'

Team leader: 'Well, I could facilitate a "5 Whys" session with the team.'

Leader: 'Great idea. Are you comfortable to give that a try, or would you like any support?'

Team leader: 'I've had the training and taken part in a few so I think I should be OK.'

Leader: 'Great. How about you give that a go and come back and let me know how it went?'

Team leader: 'Sure. How about we discuss it tomorrow afternoon?'

Leader: 'Sounds good to me. See you then.'

The temptation for the leader is to immediately dive into the detail and tell the team leader what to do about the issue. This will likely give an immediate but short-term fix; the longer-term effect is very suboptimal, however. Repeated behaviour of this nature risks building a culture of dependence: team members will stop thinking for themselves, eventually expecting all solutions to be provided by their 'boss'. Equally the leader will feel good about being able to give advice and 'fix' issues. Unfortunately, he or she will then also work very long hours, constantly firefighting and wondering why they are working so hard.

Instead, it's best to pause and focus on developing the right behaviours first rather than immediately 'fixing' the issue. This is hard, especially when a leader will often believe they know the answer. But the focus needs to shift to teaching people how to analyse problems and arrive at solutions themselves that fix the root cause. In other words, 'teach them to fish, don't just keep giving them fish'.

At the intermediate stage the organisation will have started to put in place measures to drive and monitor the use of the problem-solving tools. But a word of caution – be careful what you measure. When visiting an organisation a few years ago, one of the authors was shown the '5 Whys' problem-solving system. It was a very robust system. Standards had been agreed, templates issued and training given in how to do '5 Whys'. The expectation was clearly set that each team leader was accountable for leading '5 Whys' discussions with their team and documenting the results on the standard template. The leadership team introduced a KPI with a target on the number of '5 Whys' required from each team based on how many people where in the team. The KPI was displayed on the VMB and tracked weekly. Every team was reporting a huge number of completed '5 Why' activities, way above target. Teams beating their '5 Why' targets were publicly celebrated.

This all looked very impressive so the author then asked the site manager a question.

Coach: 'Have you seen a big reduction in the number of problems that keep recurring because of all the "5 Whys" activity?'

Site leader: 'Well, difficult to say, as we don't really have a way to measure that.'

Coach: 'OK, have any of your operational KPIs increased significantly in the last 6 months?'

Site leader (after some reflection): 'Well, not significantly. No, I can't say that they have.'

Coach: 'Did you expect them to?'

Site leader: 'Well, yes. I thought by implementing the "5 Whys" system we would significantly reduce firefighting and get an uplift on several KPIs. But neither seems to have happened.'

Coach: 'Interesting. Any idea why?'

Site leader: 'Now I reflect on it, we are getting hundreds of "5 Whys" templates completed but I'm not sure they are actually fixing the root cause. Damn. We 've been driving the wrong behaviour, haven't we?'

Coach: 'How do you mean?'

Site leader: 'We've chased the target without explaining what we really want and why it's important. We don't want lots of templates completed, we want the root cause of problems to be identified and addressed. Better to fix a smaller number than go through the motions on so many. We need to change our system.'

Coach: 'Great insight. What are you thinking? '

Site leader: 'I'm going to pull the leadership team together and we can practice what we preach by analysing the problem and doing a proper "5 Whys"!'

The result was that the target for number of '5 Whys' completed was removed and instead a measure was implemented based on the quality assessment of the '5 Whys' completed. This was based on an assessment done by the CI team who assessed a selection of completed documents each week for the quality of the analysis and the effectiveness of the solution implemented. When team are more experienced and mature the they could possible use an example where the participants knew whether they had used the correct behaviour rather than 'an expert' assessing whether they had. How many '5 Whys' resulted in an increase in performance, for example?

What's driving improvement of the coaching that the 'CI specialists' provide? The clear expectation was set that teams would have sufficient '5 Whys' for the assessment to take place. This resulted in fewer '5 Whys' being completed but a much better result with teams seeing the value of fixing the root cause and problems genuinely being solved. That is, they did not come back a few (days? weeks?) later.

ADVANCED STAGE

At the advanced stage, the organisation will have clearly established a standard system for problem solving with training and standardised processes and templates. There will be regular coaching of leaders and teams and frequent quality reviews of the effectiveness of the system. Training in the problem-solving tools and CI system will be built in as a standard element of the induction program for every new starter – at all levels.

Ideal behaviours that support the CI system will have been defined, deployed and regularly checked with KBIs. The KBIs will focus on the qualitive aspects and will be more likely to be lead indicators. Some examples could be:

- After 4–6 weeks, new starters are asked to complete a short assessment scoring how useful they found the problem-solving training in their induction and how much they have applied the learning since they joined.

- Teams rate the effective of their problem-solving sessions in a standard scoring system, e.g. top marks for very effective in ensuring problems get resolved quickly and do not reappear.

- Leaders are measured on how many problem-solving sessions they have taken part in as a participant. A regular assessment is undertaken reviewing the quality of the completed '5 Whys' and fishbones and a PDCA loop ís established for coaching and mentoring where the need is identified.

Other things that would be observed at the advanced level are that every team is using a standard approach. Easy-to-use templates are on display around VMBs and frequent problem-solving workshops are held that are focused on removing or at least reducing anything that inhibits the flow of value to the customer.

At the advanced level, everyone in the organisation would approach problem solving systematically and can demonstrate a structured approach in implementing solutions using the agreed standards. There would be regular reviews in place to determine if the system was still effective and also to examine how the system could be further improved.

KEY BEHAVIOURAL INDICATORS

Here are some examples of KBIs for CIs:

- number of problems that have recurred in the last month (testing whether we are addressing the root cause)

- number of cross-functional problem-solving workshops the team has supported (think systemically in reference to internal customers and suppliers and spreading best practice and learning)

- a simple categorisation of number of problems dealt with: Red, just done a work-around; Amber, created a short-term fix; Green, nailed the root cause. This is kept as a bar chart display.

CONTINUOUS IMPROVEMENT TAKEAWAYS

- The four main themes:

1. CI should be focused on something within the team's control and linked to the CVP or team metric

2. Huddles focused on the root cause drive employee engagement

3. Recognise completed CIs by team members that have moved team metrics

4. It's OK to start off basic then mature the complexity of CIs

- Plus 1

5. **I know how to start and mature my team's Continuous Improvements**

CONTINUOUSLY IMPROVING STANDARD OPERATING PROCEDURES

Scale	Basic			Intermediate	Advanced
	1	2	3	4	5
Standard Operating Procedures	No Standard Operating Procedures exist	Standard Operating Procedures exist, but they may not be current, complete, used or existence not known	Standard Operating Procedures exist, however they may not be followed consistently	Standard Operating Procedures exit, they are generally followed and occasionally updated	Standard Operating Procedures exist. They are consistently followed as well as reviewed and updated regularly

Figure 5.8 Maturing Standard Operating Procedures

A quick summary of the key points from Chapter 2 for SOPs:

- SOPs provide the baseline standard from which improvement can be measured and implemented

- Ensure that the people doing the work are involved in creating the SOP

- Use visual aids such as pictures, screenshots and simple flowcharts

- Make the SOP an integral part of the improvement process

HOW TO START AND MATURE SOPs

When considering Standard Operating Procedures, it is very rare that there is not something already in place. This may range from a file of flowcharts or operating instructions to a detailed Quality Manual. If we look at this in terms of maturity across the three main levels, we might typically see the following:

BEGINNER – process standards are documented and controlled through the quality management system.

INTERMEDIATE – standard operating procedures have been documented and based on the current best known practice, and improvement of the current process is actively encouraged. The SOP system is designed to make it easy to implement improvements and keep the SOPs up to date. Training in the new Standard Operating Procedure, confirmation of understanding and application of the new standard is built into the improvement cycle.

ADVANCED – in addition, SOPs would contain time targets (both elapsed time and actual work time) so that current performance can be measured against the standard and that suggested improvements can be quantified. They are proactively reviewed on a regular basis for improvement opportunities and clearly linked to any changes in the Customer Value Proposition.

Let's discuss each of these separately.

BEGINNER STAGE

So, where do we start? The first step is to understand what already exists. We can approach this in several ways depending on context and the needs of the organisation. Some organisations may choose to undertake a full in-depth review of all current processes and ensure that a documented process exists for all activities. This could be necessary in some circumstances and is likely to be a large task requiring significant time and resources. If there are no documented standards, then it's essential to start creating them. A good place to start is to quickly set priorities based on volume and risk.

In many cases, processes will already be documented to a reasonable level so let's start with the assumption that this is the case and that the organisation believes that most of the processes are being carried out in line with the current documented standard.

With this (possibly dangerous) assumption as our starting point, what kind of conversation would we like to occur when there appears to have been a mistake or there is a problem in the process? A simple question to ask is: 'Did we follow the SOP?' If the answer is 'we don't have one', then the team needs coaching in creating one. More likely is the kind of scenario below:

- Coach: 'Did we follow our standard operating procedure?'

- Team's initial attempt: 'Err – not sure.'

- Coach: 'How can we find out?'

- Team: 'Let's dig out the standard and compare what we did.'

- Coach: 'OK, great – please do that and get back to me before the end of today with your findings.'

Later the same day:

- Coach: 'What did you find?'

- Team: 'Well, we realised that a couple of the team are fairly new and aren't yet quite up to speed with the full process. This meant that we made a mistake.'

- Coach: 'OK, so what should we do?'

- Team: 'Train the new people properly.'

- Coach: 'Yes, that's definitely a good thing to do. What should we train them in?'

- Team: 'Well, the standard, of course.'

- Coach: 'OK, so do you think you could come up with a training plan that can ensure we all know the standard and how to follow it?'

- Team: 'Yes, we can do that, and then we can check that we are all working to the standard.'

- Coach: 'OK, sounds good to me. Please come up with the plan and let me know when it's been completed.'

What we are trying to do here is to ensure that everyone is at least working to the current standard. We have not looked at changing or improving the standard; the task is just to ensure that people are operating to it.

INTERMEDIATE STAGE

The key to the 'intermediate' level of maturity is a simple and effective system for managing SOPs. The system needs to designed so that the SOPs can be easily updated, training can be conducted, and SOPs can become the baseline from which further improvements can be made. Many organisations have such a system in place but it is often so onerous that people give up trying to use it.

A good system will seek to engage people actively in the process in owning their SOPs so they are a key tool for the job rather than something imposed on them by another department.

- Coach: 'Did we follow our standard operating procedure?'

- Team: 'Well, we realised that it depends. We know the standard and mainly follow it but there are times when it's easier to do something else to get the job done.'

- Coach: 'OK, so what should we do?'

- Team: 'How about we record the reasons why we can't follow the SOP every time that happens over the next couple of weeks. We'll track the data so we can understand what's stopping us from following the standard. We can then have a problem-solving meeting to discuss the data.'

- Coach: 'Sounds good to me. Please let me know what the output is of the problem-solving meeting.'

The day after the problem-solving meeting:

- Coach: 'OK, so how did it go?'

- Team: 'We collected the data and identified two scenarios where – to get the job done on time – we had to do a work-around the standard operating procedure. A couple of the most experienced team members have found an easy way to fix this but others in the team just find a way to keep the customer happy and it's easy then for mistakes to creep in or for something unexpected to happen.'

- Coach: 'I see. So, what did you decide to do?'

- Team: 'In each case we used "5 Whys" to understand the root cause as to why we couldn't follow the SOP and then we brainstormed ideas on how we might change the process to address this.'

- Coach: 'Sounds like a very good process. What have you agreed to do next?'

- Team: 'We have drafted a new SOP and discussed it with the SOP owner and QA and are going to trial it for the next 2 weeks, collect data to see if it works and then have a review meeting to discuss if the new process has fixed the issues. If it has we will confirm the new SOP, brief it out at the next huddles and ensure that everyone's trained in the changes. If not, we will go through the problem-solving cycle again and understand what we missed.'

- Coach: 'Excellent job, team. Look forward to hearing how it goes.'

What we are trying to do here is to ensure that there is a clear process for updating SOPs and that it is linked to the established problem-solving habit and integrated into the VMB and huddle habits. Of course, it is not restricted to just problems but also applies to any ideas for improvement.

ADVANCED STAGE

At the advanced stage SOPs are fully integrated in the other improvement habits. They are established as:

 » the single source of truth

 » the basis of training in the process

» having clear ownership from the teams

» having a simple and effective system in place for updating

» having a simple and effective system in place for communicating and deploying changes

» regularly reviewed for improvement opportunities

» process compliance is guided

At the advanced level, the SOPs that account for most of team's time should also include time required for each activity. The time should be both the expected elapsed time and the resource time required to complete a task.

So, for example there might be eight steps required to approve an insurance claim. The elapsed time to do this might be, say, five days and the work content time two hours. The difference is typically waiting or rework time, for example. If someone has a suggestion for improvement, then we can immediately check this suggestion against the SOP and quantify whether it will be better or worse than the current process. It may be, for example, that the Customer Value Proposition tells us we need to be able to process the claim in 48 hours. We can then analyse the current SOP and look at the opportunities to help us to achieve this.

Also, by having times on the SOPs, the team can monitor its own performance against the standards and track this on the VMB when there are identified issues or opportunities. An additional advantage is that this information can also be a very useful source of data for labour capacity planning.

Runner, Repeaters and Strangers

One common issue with SOPs is that they are often over-complicated and difficult to follow because they try to capture every possible thing that may happen in a process. So, for example, something goes wrong or a mistake happens, and so another step is added to the SOP. Before we know it, it's grown out of all recognition and no-one understands the whole thing.

One very useful technique to use to help manage this risk is the Runner, Repeater, Stranger[29] classification which helps us to classify the request type we have received. Originally developed by Lucas in the 1980s to manage production scheduling of a vast number of product variants, it is something that can be applied equally to SOPs.

- **Runner** – known demand and known frequency – typically 80% of a team's workload in terms of volume

- **Repeater** – either known demand (e.g. always get 1 of these but don't know when), or a known frequency (e.g. happens every week but don't know how many). Typically, 15 % of the number of activities

- **Stranger** – don't know how many and don't know when. Typically, less than 5% of the number of activities

If we adapt this classification to SOPs, then the SOPs should be focused on the runner and repeater activities. Trying to incorporate all stranger activities into the SOP will mean that a large proportion of the SOP will hardly ever be needed by most people. One alternative is to recognise that trying to train everyone in every possible stranger is a waste. Instead train most of the team in the runners and repeaters and have a small number of subject matter experts who can deal with

---

29 'Runners, Repeaters and Strangers', *The Blackwell Encyclopaedia of Management: Operations Management*, vol. 10, 2nd edn, eds Nigel Slack and Michael Lewis, 2015.

the strangers. That way the SOP could state 'if x happens, stop, and go to see your manager/subject matter expert'.

This will ensure the SOPs are focused on what most people must do most of the time. The SOPs will be simpler and the quality of the process outputs is thus likely to be higher.

KEY BEHAVIOURAL INDICATORS

Here are some examples of KBIs for SOPs:

- rating system of how the team value the usefulness of SOPs

- number or percentage of SOPs reviewed and improved/ simplified this month

- rating system of how easy is it to get an SOP changed/updated.

STANDARD OPERATING PROCEDURES TAKEAWAYS

- The four main themes:

1. SOPs are written instructions intended to describe how to perform tasks to achieve specific results

2. SOPs include inputs, systems, outputs, process steps, hand-offs, controls, regulatory requirements, and suppliers/ customers

3. SOPs should be ... well, standard. They should follow a prescribed standard, be held centrally, and accessible to the entire staff

4. It's OK to keep SOPs as simple as possible

- Plus 1

5. **I know how to start and mature my SOPs**

CONTINUOUSLY IMPROVING AND MATURING GEMBA WALKS

Scale	Basic			Intermediate	Advanced
	1	**2**	**3**	**4**	**5**
Go Gemba	No Go Gemba events done or Go Gemba done not in accordance with Gemba Planning Guide	Go Gemba done by team leader and as per Gemba Planning Guide	Go Gemba conducted at team leader +12 level across multiple processes and as per Gemba Planning Guide	Go Gemba conducted at Team Leader +1, +2 and +3 levels across multiple processes as per Gemba Planning Guide	Go Gemba conducted at all levels including senior management and as per Gemba Planning Guide

Figure 5.9 Maturing Gemba walks

A quick summary of the key points from Chapter 2 for Gemba walks:

- They should not be introduced as a separate activity or stand-alone 'tool' and instead bring most value when visibly integrated into the overall System of Improvement and the System of Thinking and Behaviour

- They provide a process to coach and develop people's skills by recognising that the role of leaders is to serve the workforce to better enable the workforce to serve the customer

- An effective Gemba walk will leave leaders, managers and associates feeling valued.

We cannot do full justice to the topic of Gemba walks in this book. Rather we hope to highlight the key points, show why they are so powerful and how they are essential to the development and sustainment of a continuous improvement culture. Jim Lancaster, CEO, Lantech, puts it succinctly: 'I have always had a problem convincing CEOs of one simple thing. They need to take the time to go where value is created. They need to learn to see the work and to see how their management system utterly fails to support the daily work. My most important advice is to screw up your courage, put aside your daily distractions, and walk out into the work to see how value is created at the frontline.'

For those wishing to dive more deeply into understanding Gemba walks we highly recommend Michael Bremer's Shingo Prize winning book *How to do a Gemba Walk – A Leader's Guide*.

Gemba walks need to be a key part of any leader's standard work not only because they are so powerful for checking on and embedding the CI habits but also because they provide an ideal opportunity to practice the desired leadership behaviours.

In 2015 Dr Joe Folkman published an industry white paper entitled '9 Vital Leadership Behaviours that boost Employee Productivity' based on a research study of 'almost 100,000 direct reports in hundreds of different organisations. Each direct report rated the effectiveness of his or her immediate manager and the level of satisfaction/ commitment each had with the organization. The effectiveness of leaders was assessed by 49 behavioural items which evaluated 16 leadership competencies.'

From all the different leadership behaviours that were assessed, nine key leadership behaviours that had the biggest positive impact on employee's engagement were identified. These behaviours, with short extracts from the full paper, are reproduced below with the kind permission of Dr Folkman. If we reflect on each of these behaviours the Gemba walk provides the opportunity to demonstrate and practice all of them. This is one of the reasons they are so powerful.

1. **Inspire and Motivate Others** – 'Leaders who are effective at inspiring and motivating others have a high level of energy and enthusiasm. They energize their team to achieve difficult goals and increase the level of performance from everyone on the team.'

2. **Driving for Results** – 'The drive for results is a critical behaviour to success ... Leaders who are effective at driving for results are skilful at getting people to stay focused on and stretch for the highest priority goals.'

3. **Strategic Perspective** – 'Leaders who provide their team with a definite sense of direction and purpose tend to have more satisfied and committed employees. These leaders paint a clear perspective between the overall picture and the details of day-to-day activities.'

4. **Collaboration** – 'Leaders who promote a high level of cooperation between their work group and other groups create a positive and productive atmosphere in the organization. When leaders demonstrate that they can achieve objectives that require a high level of inter-group cooperation, synergy is created and every employee enjoys the work experience.'

5. **Walk the Talk** – 'A key behaviour in creating a satisfied and committed workforce is the very basic and fundamental skill of being honest and acting with integrity. Leaders need to be role models and set a good example for their work group.'

6. **Trust** – 'Leaders can engender trust by becoming aware of the concerns, aspirations, and circumstances of others.'

7. **Develops and Supports Others** – 'When leaders work with employees and push them to develop new skills and abilities, they are building higher levels of employee satisfaction and commitment.'

8. **Building Relationships** – 'Leaders who stay in touch with issues and concerns of individuals in the work group have employees with higher levels of employee satisfaction and commitment.'

9. **Courage** –'The leaders with the highest levels of employee satisfaction and commitment are courageous. It takes courage to address issues, resolve conflicts, and insist that everyone is accountable.

This list could be used as a simple self-check list.[30]

Gemba walks provide the opportunity for leaders to understand how well the organisation has embedded the habits. They provide the opportunity to test the effectiveness of the deployment of the systems of improvement and thinking and behaviour. They are in no way meant to be used to test or assess the individuals or teams visited but rather test how well the systems have enabled the desired knowledge and behaviours. The Gemba walks are intended to support, promote and check on the other habits.

HOW TO START AND MATURE GEMBA WALKS

A good Gemba walk is something that takes a lot of practice. Gemba walks help leaders to distinguish between Process and People. For example: 'Why was the Process not capable of handling this situation?'

It should help people understand it's not about 'who to blame'. Gemba walks are what Toyota describes as *Genchi Genbutsu* – 'going to the source to find the facts to make correct decisions, build consensus, and achieve goals'.[31]

If we look at this in terms of maturity across the three main levels, we might typically see the following:

BEGINNER – The organisation has recognised that Gemba walks are important and has set a clear expectation that leaders at all levels should do them.

---

30   Joe Folkman, *9 VITAL LEADERSHIP BEHAVIORS THAT BOOST EMPLOYEE PRODUCTIVITY: The keys to increasing discretionary effort,* The Clemmer Group, 2015.

31   Michael Bremer, *How to do a Gemba Walk – A Leader's Guide.* 2017

INTERMEDIATE – Leaders have been trained in how to do Gemba walks and they are recognised as an integral element of the System of Improvement and the System of Thinking and Behaviour. Key Behaviour Indicators are being experimented with.

ADVANCED – Gemba walks are regularly reviewed for effectiveness with leaders honing their skills in shared 'lessons learned' reviews. They are part of all leaders' standard work and valued by both leaders and employees across the organisation. Key Behaviour Indicators are well established and in place to measure and track effectiveness.

Let's discuss each of these in more detail separately.

BEGINNER STAGE

For some leaders, Gemba walks come naturally and they are probably already doing something similar but not necessarily in a structured way. For others, a Gemba walk may represent a completely different way of leading that they are very uncomfortable with. So, the starting point is to explain why the organisation believes Gemba walks are important and to set clear expectations about what their purpose is and what good looks like. It's also important that they are not begun as a stand-alone task but are seen a part of the overall System of Improvement.

Rather than start everywhere at once, let those who naturally take to the approach lead the initial walks as part of a roll-out plan, encourage participation at all levels, and establish formal shared learning sessions on what makes a good walk. Ideally, take video footage of some good examples and use these for promotion and learning. Senior executives need to lead by example and make themselves highly visible practising Gemba walks.

Michael Bremer describes the key elements of a good Gemba walk as:

1. Setting direction with challenging targets

2. Learning to more effectively see problems, abnormalities, waste and opportunities

These are good objectives to set at the beginner stage. Bremer also suggests a simple model to structure a Gemba walk which is illustrated below:

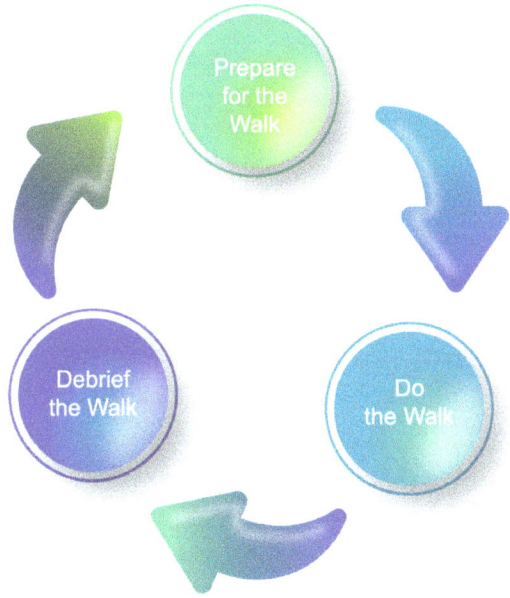

Figure 5.10 Gemba walk model

INTERMEDIATE STAGE

At the intermediate stage Gemba walks have been well established and the key elements outlined above of setting direction with challenging targets and learning to more effectively see problems, abnormalities, waste and opportunities are in place.

At this stage, we would aim to have a 'great Gemba walk'[32] which, as Bremer goes on to describe, would also:

---

32 Mike Rother, *Toyota Kata: Managing People for Improvement, Adaptiveness and Superior Results,* McGraw-Hill, 2010.

1. Teach/coach associates to develop their ability to perform and to fix and improve their processes

2. Have the tenacity to stay on course, yet balance that drive with a humility that permits them to stay in touch with reality as it exists

3. Align support systems to elevate the organisation's improvement maturity

At this stage organisations will often have measures and targets in place around the frequency and number of walks leaders should do. However, what's often missing are measures around the effectiveness of the Gemba walks which is one of the key elements needed to move to the advanced level.

While it's useful and important to establish expectations around frequency and number of walks and start building these into a leader's standard work, it's critical that these measures don't just encourage 'tick the box' exercises. This will result in lots of activity being reported but little benefit derived from the time invested. To avoid this, the leader needs to be coached in the type of conversation needed.

In his Shingo Prize winning book *Toyota Kata*, Michael Rother explains a very similar approach used at Toyota and suggests leaders use five key questions to help them structure the conversation. These are:

- 'What is the target condition?' (the challenge)

- 'What is the actual condition now?'

- 'What obstacles are now preventing you from reaching the target condition? Which one are you addressing now?'

- 'What is your next step?'

- 'When can we go and see what we have learned from taking that step?'

At the intermediate stage, we would expect leaders to be thinking about these questions and practising their application in every conversation on every Gemba walk.

An example of a typical conversation that could take place at this stage and the advanced stage is given below.

- Team leader: 'I would just like to welcome Max to our huddle. For those of you who have not met him Max is VP of R&D and is doing a Gemba walk in Operations today and has asked to observe our huddle. Welcome, Max.'

- Max: 'Hi everyone. Many thanks for the opportunity to learn from your huddle.'

Huddle is conducted with good interaction and discussion and is completed in ten minutes.

- Team leader: 'Many thanks, everyone. Max, do you have any questions?'

- Max: 'Yes, thanks. Just to help me understand I see you have two KPIs in orange and I wondered what that means?'

- Team leader: 'Kelly, would like to explain the process we are working to.'

- Kelly: 'Sure. If something's in orange, then it means it's not on target but we have a plan to get it back on target. On our PDCA section on the board you can see two actions in the "check" section. These are related to the KPIs. We have implemented actions following problem-solving session and are now testing the solutions. As soon as the solution has been tested we will move it to the "do" section to show that it's implemented. Once we've proven that it works to get us back on target we will remove it from the PDCA board and make the KPI green.'

- Max: 'That's a great system. I would like to see if we can use that in R&D. Would you mind coming over and explaining it to some of our team leaders?'

- Kelly: 'Sure. But it would be even better if they could come here and I could show it to them and talk them through it.'

- Max: 'Great idea. I will ask them to make contact and fix something up. I notice that there is also a KPI in red. What's the story there?'

- Team leader: 'Well, it's in red if we are not on target and we don't have an agreed action plan to fix it.'

- Max: 'I see. So why wouldn't you have an action plan?'

At this point, there is awkward silence, foot shuffling and avoidance of eye contact from various team members. This is a critical point in the Gemba walk discussion. The key is to avoid jumping in with a suggestion or another string of questions. Instead smile politely and wait.

- Team leader: 'Well, the thing is we are struggling with this because the root cause is that we are not getting information we need from team x in R&D on time.'

- Max: 'I see. Have you raised the issue with them?'

- Team leader: 'Yes. Several times. And we have an agreed service level agreement for response time but they are very busy with other priorities.'

- Max: 'So what's the implications of it being in red?'

- Team leader: 'It means we can't hit our agreed target response rate to the customer which is a key element in the Customer Value Proposition.'

- Max: 'Do the guys in team x understand why it's important from the customer's perspective?'

- Team leader: 'Umm. Probably not.'

- Max: 'Anyone have any suggestions on how we might make progress on this?'

- Kelly: 'How about the team leader of team x comes over and I talk them through our PDCA system and explain why this KPI is so important to the customer? We could also offer to host a joint problem-solving activity to come up with a shared plan.'

- Max: 'Great suggestion. I'll ask the team x team leader to tie up with you and will check back in with you and them in a couple of weeks. Many thanks for your time guys. It's been a really interesting and useful discussion.'

The conversation here is trying to use the 'enquiry-based' coaching approach, where leaders seek to embed learning through asking meaningful questions rather than just giving advice. This is key to a successful Gemba walk.

ADVANCED STAGE

At the advanced level Gemba walks are well established and have become recognised as a key element of standard work for all leaders. They are not seen as an extra task but rather as a key enabler to getting the job done. At this level, it is about embedding Gemba walks as a standard across the organisation, ensuring that people are trained in how to conduct the right kind of 'enquiry-based' conversations.

The leaders will regularly review the effectiveness of both the walk and the system that is in place to drive and support them. Leaders will act with humility and recognise that with every walk they are honing their skills and will actively participate in shared 'lessons learned' reviews with peers.

Gemba walks should add real value both to leaders and employees and to the organisation. Typically, we see organisations implementing measures around the frequency and number of walks leaders should do but at the advanced stage we also need to implement Key Behavioural Indicators (KBIs) to monitor the effectiveness of Gemba walks. At the advanced stage, the KBIs are well established and in place to measure and track effectiveness but are also being constantly reviewed and checked to ensure they are driving the ideal behaviour.

There is no list of 'correct' KBIs that will work in every organisation. They need to be context-specific and designed and changed to reflect the current reality. That said, here are a couple of examples that other organisations are using.

The senior executives in one organisation wanted the associates to hold the executives accountable for doing Gemba walks so they encouraged teams to come up with creative ways to do this. One day a couple of weeks later the CEO was surprised to see photographs of the executive team members had appeared on several visual management boards. Some photos had a big green dot on them and others did not. She paused at one of the VMBs and asked a team member about them.

CEO: 'I like the photos. Why do some have a green dot and others don't?'

Team member: 'Well, anyone with a green dot is someone who has visited the team in the last two weeks. No green dot means we haven't seen them for a while.'

CEO: 'Fantastic idea. Please share it on the internal network.'

In another example, one organisation had a rigorous KPI system in place for ensuring that managers had completed the target number of Gemba walks and this KPI was visibly displayed in a league table. This led to some undesirable behaviours as it became a bit of a competition to be top of the league, and being in the top five achievers in terms of number of walks became more important than how effective the walks were. This eventually challenged the whole credibility of the Gemba system as it became a 'tick the box' exercise and was more about the leaders' egos than about what it was intended to achieve. So, a cross-functional team of employees was asked to come up with ideas on different ways to measure the Gemba walks. They trialled a few things but eventually rolled out an anonymous version of a Net Promoter Score (NPS). The simple question was 'did you get real value out of the last conversation you engaged in as part of a Gemba walk?' Importantly both the leaders doing walks and associates experiencing them were asked to complete the quick online rating system. These NPS results are an important KBI.

Final tip for Gemba walks – as with many things the key to their effectiveness is not **what** we do but **how** we do it.

Key Behavioural Indicators

Here are some examples of KBIs for Gemba walks:

- number of Gemba learning reviews conducted by managers in peer groups (i.e. how can we do walks better?)

- the green dot on photographs of leaders who have visited the team as in the example above

- a Net Promoter Score system that tracks how people rate the quality and effectiveness of conversations undertaken during Gemba walks

GEMBA WALKS TAKEAWAYS

- The four main themes:

1. Gemba is a process of discovery ... have an open mind and maintain curiosity throughout. It is never about validating preconceptions, but rather discovering what is going on.

2. Prepare ahead so that you concentrate on observation. A good place to start is by reading the SOP to learn the language and the process, and you can catch people doing what they're supposed to be doing!

3. Maintain respect for those working on the process who understand it best. Engage people by directly listening, seeing, and resist the temptation to jump in with answers.

4. It's OK to start off at a basic level, then mature the Gemba walks

- Plus 1

5. **I know how to start and mature my Gemba walks**

NEUROSCIENCE OF BUILDING HABITS

Charles Duhiggs[33] identifies the neuroscience and psychology related to developing habits and promoting good habits and breaking bad habits. He discusses the basal ganglia and the brain stem that are the same regions of the brain where habits reside. The habit-making behaviours relate to a part of the brain called the basal ganglia, which also plays a key role in the development of emotions, memories and pattern recognition. Interestingly, decisions are made in a different part of the brain called the prefrontal cortex. Habits are sometimes

---

33 Charles Duhiggs, *The Neuroscience of Habits: how they form and how to change them,* Scientific American, 27 April 2012.

compulsory. New behaviours can become automatic through the process of habit formation. Old habits are hard to break and new habits are hard to form because the behavioural patterns that humans repeat become imprinted in neural pathways, but it is possible to form new habits through repetition. The key is repetition and positive reinforcement for trying.

The second important element of forming new habits is the element of choice. When individuals feel they have a choice, this allows the brain to avoid a stressed state. Provided the environment is positive, they are willing to try something new and be vulnerable enough to perhaps not get it quite right and possibly fail. To help the brain create new pathways it tries to transfer processing from the prefrontal cortex to the basal ganglia, i.e. subconsciously This requires simplifying and repetition of the habits while accepting good enough results, not necessarily perfection. Duhiggs also suggests that when individuals choose to adapt and evolve the habit, then the brain not only modifies the wiring of the habit, it reinforces the neuropathy. So basically, this technique is giving people the power to rewire their brains and create new habits.

The brain is not the stable, unchanging structure one might imagine. It's dynamic and changeable; a characteristic called neuroplasticity. In fact, neuroplasticity is going on all the time in our brains. As brain scientists like to say, 'Any time you do something you're more likely to do it again.' In other words, actions and behaviours that we repeat, intentionally or unintentionally, can get woven into the neural structures of our brain. Whatever we focus on and repeatedly do with enthusiasm tends to become our preferred way of thinking and acting; our mindset and habits. This is one way we develop our patterns of thinking and behaviour. It's also a way we can deliberately modify our thinking and behaviour patterns. Practicing the Habits is a good example.

The organisational culture reinforces and perpetuates itself daily. But as we know from sports and music, with the following ingredients we can rewire our brains to acquire new skills and habits:

- structured routines for beginners to practice,

- frequent repetition,

- feedback from a coach to correct our practice, and

- optimism from feeling that we're overcoming obstacles and making progress.

Some points to remember:

- The brain learns to favour whatever we focus on repeatedly. As this information is reinforced through repetition it becomes wired in the brain and solidifies our thoughts and actions. It becomes who you are.

- Due to these preferred pathways in the brain we are led into using them again and again, which strengthens them even more.

- It is possible to alter our mindset! A way to rewire the brain is to deliberately practice a new pattern. In so doing the existing pathways lose their strength and are replaced with other neural pathways and behaviours.

- A sense of optimism will be important. To develop new habits and a sense of self-efficacy through practice, the learner should experience successes and the positive emotions that come from them.

In martial arts and in the Toyota Kata,[34] a kata is any structured way of thinking and acting that you practice until the pattern becomes a habit. Through practicing, the pattern of behaviour becomes second nature; so that you just 'do what you do' with little or no conscious

---

34 Mike Rother, *Toyota Kata: Managing People for Improvement, Adaptiveness and Superior Results*, McGraw-Hill, 2010.

attention. These patterns provide field-proven, teachable, repeatable model ways of thinking and acting when faced with different types of situations commonly encountered in your real-world work environment. There are two kata patterns, however, that provide an overarching methodology that can serve as a background pattern within which all other lean tools and methods are used. These are the two kata patterns taught by Mike Rother in his book, *Toyota Kata*:[35]

1. the Improvement Kata

2. the Coaching Kata

The Improvement Kata is fundamentally the PDCA, as the most important way to truly embed the new habits is through positive reinforcement using the Coaching Kata, which we have tried to demonstrate in the coaching conversations in this chapter.

MATURING HABITS TAKEAWAYS

1. It is OK to start out with something basic

2. Have the mindset that you can always improve each habit

3. Get feedback from a coach and your customers on how you can mature and challenge the team's thinking

4. Go Gemba to see how others are progressing with the habits and see what you can learn from them

- Plus 1

5. **Always seeking to improve each habit almost becomes another habit.**

---

35 Mike Rother, *Toyota Kata: Managing People for Improvement, Adaptiveness and Superior Results*, McGraw-Hill, 2010.

CHAPTER 6

IT DEPENDS ...

It's not just tools or individual capability but an organisation's culture that's critical.

There is no standard off-the-shelf answer to creating a culture of continuous improvement. There are several key things that can increase the chances of success, and defining ideal behaviours and habits that reinforce these behaviours is one of these.

However, there is no single answer to the question, 'Which are the right habits for each particular organisation?' nor to 'What is the one and only sure-fire way of ensuring a successful implementation?' The fact is that each organisation is different. They have different cultures, different leadership styles, different priorities, and different people. So, while what is needed can be identified, the specific behaviours and habits that improve the chances of success are very context-specific ones. The answer to nearly every question of the detail is 'It depends'.

That said, there are several things that can be done to help increase the probability of success and the aim of this chapter is to share these insights.

Many organisations spend months having a central improvement team develop a set of training materials, how-to guides and in-depth manuals around the agreed toolset.

None of the tools are bad and lots of the material is of high quality and delivered by excellent trainers. However, in almost every case the only variation has been how long it takes for the use of the tools to fade away and become discredited yet another failed initiative.

Applying the Plan, Do, Check, Act cycle requires going back to plan and considering why this is and what needs to be done differently. The answer is not to repeat the same mistake by developing a different toolset, getting even better, glossier training material or even more experienced trainers. Nor will changing the name help.

The Shingo model teaches us that an organisation's leadership team needs to define the desired culture. To make that organisational culture tangible, the leaders need to define the ideal behaviours that will be visible. This is different from defining values. Unfortunately, many great values fail to get embedded across organisations because people struggle to relate to them on a day-to-day basis.

Unless they are defined in clear, observable behaviours the danger is they just become statements of intent. Everyone agrees they are great values but few people live and breathe them every day. Defining behaviours that everyone can observe, check and give feedback on means that it is much more likely that the desired culture will be realised.

However, behaviour on its own is not enough. We can define and deploy ideal behaviours but if the tools and systems do not support these behaviours then the desired culture is likely to not be achieved.

The Shingo model teaches us that the desired culture needs to be supported by the right tools and systems. The organisation needs to ensure that all tools and systems are aligned to the ideal behaviours.

The model below, adapted from *Staying Lean* by Peter Hines et al., shows some of the consequences of not having aligned tools, systems and behaviours.

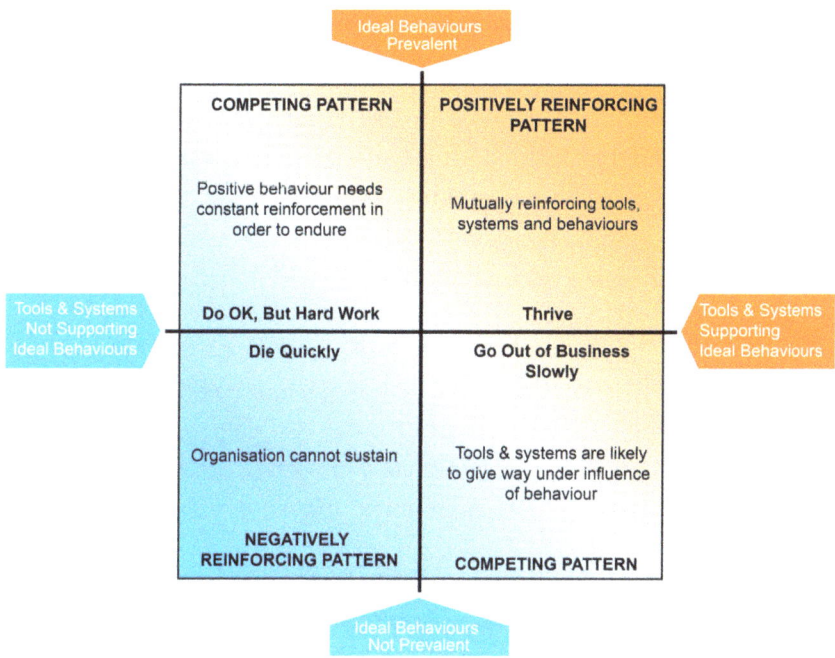

Figure 6.1 Matrix of tools/systems vs ideal behaviours

The three key insights from the Shingo model for Enterprise Excellence are:

1. Ideal results require ideal behaviour.

2. Beliefs and systems drive behaviour.

3. Principles inform behaviour.

The habits are informed by the principles; by continuously reinforcing the systems, they help embed the ideal behaviours. Many lessons continue to be learned in the attempts to apply the Shingo model teachings but one that this book seeks to share is that defining a set of simple habits was a very effective way to embed the desired behaviours.

THE ROADMAP

Shingo teaches us that every organisation needs to start with defining the culture to which it aspires. In these case studies the desired organisational culture was one of continuous improvement – always seeking to make tomorrow a better experience for customers and our people. A simple high-level implementation roadmap that any organisation can use is shown below:

1. Initially, the leadership team needs to define the ideal behaviours that will visibly demonstrate the desired culture. For example, one element of the desired culture could be that everyone in the organisation is a proactive problem solver using structured problem-solving tools every day.

2. Then for each desired high-level behaviour, decide what is the habit or habits that will drive and embed this behaviour. A single habit could drive several behaviours.

3. Once the habits have been defined, the next step is to define and create the learning system that will embed them.

4. Simultaneously ensure that the desired behaviours are clearly articulated, understood and embedded into the organisation's leadership at every level and that people are given the opportunity to explore and understand what these behaviours mean and how they will be demonstrated

In this way, the behaviours are visibly demonstrated through the application of the habits. But it does not stop there. Constant practice and application of the habits reinforce the desired behaviours. Thus, we create a circle of ever deeper understanding of the habits and widespread application of the desired behaviours.

It is good practice to apply Plan, Do, Check, Act to the roll-out of the habits. Some key points to consider in each phase are:

PLAN

How will the organisation ensure the habits and desired behaviours are important to the leadership population? In the case studies provided earlier, this was done by ensuring the highest-level executives proactively lived and breathed the habits and behaviours. The key was ensuring that the reward and recognition system was linked to the habits and behaviours. Lead indicators were deployed around the application and depth of understanding of the habits in each team with clear targets and accountability from the leaders.

It is always a choice whether to implement any change as a 'Big Bang' company-wide approach or a phased introduction. There is not a right or wrong approach – it is a context-specific decision and needs careful consideration of the advantages and disadvantages in each case. In truth, it depends.

Should the approach be to launch all habits at once, as in the Bank of New York Mellon examples, or have a phased implementation, as was the case in the Commonwealth Bank? Again, there is no fixed, magic answer to this. It depends on the context.

Review, agree and clearly define what Key Performance Indicators will be used and very importantly what the Key Behavioural Indicators will be. Ensure there is a rigorous PDCA cycle in place that regularly reviews these indicators as it is extremely likely that they will need to be refined or changed as lessons are learned.

Make sure there is clear agreement on the governance structure, sponsorship and reporting lines and keep it simple.

DO

Ensure the CEO and executive leaders passionately support an agreed culture they aspire to for the organisation. This may take some time but it is essential that this is clearly articulated and shared by the leadership team.

It is important that the behaviours are not defined by a small expert team behind closed doors who suddenly reveal the answers as a big surprise. A wide cross-section of people need to be involved in developing the desired behaviours and habits and the language used to describe them needs to be engaging for everyone.

Implement the plan with constant mini PDCA cycles are every stage. Be prepared to change and refine as lessons are learned. Explain from the start that continuous improvement will be applied to the continuous improvement approach.

An often-neglected area is that of teaching leaders how to coach in a CI culture. Enquiry-based (or Kata) coaching requires a lot of practice and is very different from traditional coaching. Leaders will need training and coaching support in the habits and desired behaviours and they will need help in understanding how to coach these with their people.

And don't forget to constantly communicate, communicate, communicate even if you are just communicating the same message.

CHECK

Be prepared to listen to feedback and adjust as appropriate. Casting everything in stone and refusing to change when the data is telling us something is not working is going to guarantee failure.

Often our existing systems or processes either don't support the desired behaviour or they even drive the opposite behaviour. This will become apparent through the application of the habits. So, encourage teams at all levels to flag up instances where an existing system/process is contradictory to the desired behaviours and use the application of the habits to address the issues. This may mean that an issue must be escalated if it cannot be resolved at a local level and needs to progress through the governance structure. Some of the more obvious issues can be identified in the planning phase and be addressed, but be prepared that there are likely to be several surprises.

Review KPIs and KBIs on a regular basis, not only progress towards them and whether the targets need adjusting, but also to validate whether they are still the right ones. They are likely to need to change as the maturity of the habits and behaviours change.

ACT

Broaden (horizontally across all departments) and deepen (vertically to all levels) the application of the habits. Constantly review how widespread they are across different parts of the organisation and how far through the layers are they being applied.

Ensure leaders have set clear targets for the application of the habits, that an agreed measurement process is in place to monitor and support progress, and that coaching is designed to help increase the chances of success.

It's important to get the balance right between being overly prescriptive and allowing freedom and creativity. Too much prescription (command and control) leads to lack of engagement and no matter how great the habits they will not be sustainable. Too much freedom and the core idea of the habits will be lost and will eventually be discredited as people can no longer recognise a common approach.

Celebrate success all the time. It is far better to have lots of small celebrations and constant reminders than to have one big annual event.

NEUROSCIENCE BEHIND THREATS AND REWARDS

Fear of change is something we all must varying degrees, and we all deal with it differently. Some people accept the change immediately, some will take some time, whilst others never quite get to even accepting the change.

Change is never easy, even in small amounts and we all will try to avoid some change. Interestingly, we need to change how we think about change.[40] If we think it is being imposed on us we will tend to resist, whereas if we are part of coming up with the change ourselves then this resistance tends to either disappear or dramatically reduce. So why talk about change in this book? The simplicity and fundamentals of the 4 core habits are around individual's realising a need for change, coming up with potential ideas for the change, implementing the solution and then seeing the improvements and often being positively acknowledged by peers and the management for implementing the change. Chris Ortiz[41] talks about how successful leaders in small to medium enterprises find it difficult to let to and delegate completion of tasks and solving problems. It is not just about delegating tasks but releasing the emotional attachments and letting others improve those elements that are hurting or holding back the business's ability to improve.

Having a stand-up 10-15-minute huddle where different team members can run the huddle, and acknowledging or positively rewarding peers on great behaviours during change, creates a safe environment whilst embedding the behaviours as individual habits.

40 Interview with Jon Pratlett, 11 January 2017, www.JonPratlett.com.
41 C.A. Ortiz, *The Psychology of Lean Improvements*, CRC Press, 2012.

At this point, it is timely to refer to David Rock's SCARF model. Safety is key for the brain! As previously mentioned in Chapter 1, the brain reacts adversely to threats. It is vital to run a SCARF scan through all proposed changes and consider potential threats and how they might be mitigated and rewards enhanced. Bear in mind the brain is considered by some social neuroscientists as five times more sensitive to threat than reward – we run away from threat and walk toward reward. Threat responses are longer lasting, faster acting, stronger and more common. Reward responses are slower acting, milder, shorter and less common. Hence, as leaders, we need to encourage people to savour the wins (increasing the duration and intensity of them). A true understanding of how people's brains work and hence their behaviours is critical if one wants to create alignment to a standard set of behaviours. The work of John Medina[42] and David Rock examined the development and study of habits that drive desired behaviours that collectively create a culture of continuous improvement.

1. The brain is a connection machine

2. No two human brains are alike

3. The brain has a constrained conscious processing capability

4. The brain does not unlearn

5. Stressed brains don't learn or listen

---

42   John Medina, *Brain Rules,* Pear Press, 2008.

CHAPTER TAKEAWAYS

- The four main themes

1. Habits embed BEHAVIOURS

2. The right HABITS drive the right BEHAVIOURS

3. MEASURING the right HABITS increases CI MATURITY

4. Continuously lifting EXPECTATIONS around HABITS delivers SUSTAINABILITY

- Plus1

5. **HABITS drive the right BEHAVIOURS that deliver the right CUSTOMER EXPERIENCE, highly engaged people and sustainable business RESULTS.**

REFERENCES

Alexandre, Dalceri Sternadt & Tavares, João Manuel R. S., *Introduction of Human Perception in Visualization*, 2006. https://web.fe.up.pt/~tavares/downloads/publications/artigos/IJI_Manuscript_DA_ JT.pdf

Blackford, Mansel G., Bridgestone Tyres example in *The Rise of Modern Business*, University of North Carolina Press, 2008.

Boston Consulting Group, *Lean that Lasts – Transforming Financial Institutions*, September 2012.

Chakravorty, Satya, 'Where Process Improvement Projects Go Wrong', Wall Street International, 25 January 2010.

Covey, Stephen, *The 7 Habits of Highly Effective People*.

Dinero, Donald, *Training Within Industry: The Foundation of Lean. Productivity Press, Portland, Oregon, 2005.*

Doidge, Norman, M.D., *The Brain That Changes Itself*, Penguin Books, New York, 2007.

Duhiggs, Charles, 'The Neuroscience of Habits: how they form and how to change them', *Scientific American*, 27 April 2012.

Green, R., *The Persuasive Properties of Colour*, Marketing Communications, 1998.

Hansen, Kristen, *TRACTION: The Neuroscience of Leadership*, enhansenperformance.com.au, 2017.

Harder, Brenton, Case for Operational Excellence Program, plan submitted to Executive Committee of a large financial institution in support of a 4+1 program (scope and scale modified for illustration purposes), Nov. 2012.

Hines, Peter, Found, Pauline, Griffiths, Gary & Harrison, Richard, *Staying Lean: Thriving, Not Just Surviving*, CRC Press, New Jersey, 2008.

171

Kotter, John P., *Leading Change: Why Transformation Efforts Fail*, HBR OnPoint, 2000.

Kotter, John P., 'The 8-Step Process for Leading Change', http://www. kotterinternational.com/the-8-step-process-for-leading-change/, 2017.

Langer, Ellen, Russell, Timothy & Eisenkraft, Noah, 'Orchestral performance and the footprint of mindfulness', *Psychology of Music*, Vol. 37, No. 2, 2009.

Levie, W. J. & Lentz, R., *Effects of text illustrations: A review of research*, Educational Communication and Technology, 1982.

Medina, John, *Brain Rules*, Pear Press, 2008.

Ortiz, C.A., *The Psychology of Lean Improvements*, CRC Press, 2012.

Pietersen, Willie, *The Journal of Business Strategy*, Columbia Business School.

Pratlett, Jon, interview, 11 January 2017. www.JonPratlett.com.

Regelman, Roman, Bartletta, Simon, Duthoit, Christophe, Letorneux, Yann & Roig, Victoria, *Lean that Lasts – Transforming Financial Institutions*,Boston Consulting Group, Boston, 2012.

Rock, David, SCARF Model, *NeuroLeadership Journal*, 2008.

Rock, David, *Your Brain at Work: Strategies for Overcoming Distraction, Regaining Focus, and Working Smarter All Day Long*, Wiley Press, New Jersey, 2009.

Rock, David, *Coaching with the Brain in Mind*, Wiley Press, New Jersey, 2009.

Schein, Edgar, cited in Ch. 19, *WCOM (World Class Operations Management): Why You Need More Than Lean*, Carlo Baroncelli and Noela Ballerio (eds), Springer, 2016.

Slack, Nigel & Lewis, Michael (eds), 'Runners, Repeaters and Strangers', *The Blackwell Encyclopaedia of Management: Operations Management*, vol. 10, 2nd edn, 2015.

Stapp, H., Schwartz, J.M. & Beauregard, M., *Quantum theory in neuroscience and psychology: A neurophysical model of mind–brain interaction*, Philosophical Transactions of the Royal Society of London, 2005.

The Karate Kid, Columbia Pictures, 1984.

Toseland, Ronald W. and Rivas, Robert F., *An Introduction to Group Work Practice*, Allyn & Bacon/ Longman, Boston, 2005.

Other sources

Details on Shingo Model can be found on www.shingo.org

Details on S A Partners can be found on www.sapartners.com

ABOUT THE AUTHORS

The authors have collectively over 70 years' experience in business improvement.

Morgan started off as a naval officer specialising in engineering, then undertook a master's degree in Lean. He has deployed Lean Six Sigma in over seven different organisations, training over 1000 black belts, 5000 green belts and coaching the delivery of over $1bn in savings and over 23 international awards. He works in many industry sectors including automotive, marine, heavy engineering, government, logistics and financial services. He has a PhD in competitive advantage and technology diffusion and is a certified executive coach and published author.

Chris Butterworth has had many years' experience of operating at senior management positions in several multinational organisations such as JCB, Jaguar and Corus and has been a partner with S A Partners for over sixteen years. Chris coach's executive teams and transfers knowledge across all levels of an organisation and has spoken at many international conferences. He is a certified Shingo Institute facilitator, a Shingo examiner and winner of Best New Speaker of the Year Award for TEC- The Executive Connection.

After serving ten years as an F/A-18 fighter pilot in the US Marines, Brenton Harder moved to London as Head of Quality and IT with General Electric Information Services. Several years later, he moved to New York with HSBC as Senior VP for Global Transaction Banking before moving to Boston and Bangalore, India with Fidelity Investments as Head of Service Integration. Zurich was next for four years as Head of Operational Excellence with Credit Suisse, followed by another four years in Sydney leading the Business Productivity Group for the Commonwealth Bank of Australia. Brent is back in the USA now as Head of Business Process Improvement with the Bank of New York Mellon. He is a Certified Master Black Belt from GE, and holds a MBA, and a MSc in Technology Management.

Lightning Source UK Ltd.
Milton Keynes UK
UKHW02f1754130818
327172UK00009B/185/P